MW01351834

146/300

Written by Nicholas Beatty
Illustrated by Coleen McIntyre

Contributing Editor, Rachelle Matheson
Contributing Editor, Sophie Albright

BOOK Sprocket

BookSprocket.com
3439 NE Sandy Blvd #305
Portland, OR 97232

- Text and illustrations by Nicholas Beatty and Coleen McIntyre
- Edited by Pamela Ellgen
- Book design and layout by Mykal Murphree and Marta Royo : Watson Creative

Dedication:

Nicholas Beatty: *The Cultured Chef* is dedicated to my parents Richard & Darlene Beatty, and my partner Mark Middleton. Your love and encouragement means everything!

Coleen McIntyre: I would like to dedicate this book to my awesome parents, Jeannie and Dave McIntyre - and to everyone else along the way that believed in me.

At BookSprocket, philanthropy is a core component of our culture. Our founders have a rich history of giving back to the arts and cultural organizations serving children in poor communities around the world. A portion of sales from The Cultured Chef will be donated to our non-profit partner Ayudame a Pintar Mi Futuro in San Pedro la Laguna, Guatemala. (PaintmyFuture.info)

ISBN: 978-0-9914770-0-5
Library of Congress Control Number: 2014902026
Printed and Bound in China

INTRODUCTION

For as long as I can remember, I have been fascinated by world cultures. The spark was first ignited during visits to the library where I found beautiful illustrations and photographs of distant cities. From then on, my parents and teachers went out of their way to help encourage my passion for learning about life in other countries.

The Cultured Chef is the kind of book I would have loved as a child. It brings to life the sights, sounds, colors and flavors experienced when visiting a foreign country for the first time.

My creative partner Coleen McIntyre and I have spent thousands of hours reading about other cultures, testing recipes and even visiting many of the places represented in this book. Our hope was to create a book that not only educates but also inspires young people to develop a global perspective and a new way of life. I truly believe that this is the key to success for future generations.

We invite you to share this book with the curious children in your life.

Nicholas Beatty

We're offering a treasure chest full of free activities, fun information and a 30-minute audio book. Simply go to our website www.CulturedChef.com/key and begin your adventure by typing in the code found on the skeleton key on this page.

Kids: Read this First

Thank you for checking out our book! We've included hundreds of pictures of really cool people and places from around the world just for you. You can read the stories one at a time, try the recipes with an adult and listen to our audio book online. In addition, we've provided two surprises for you below. We hope you enjoy ***The Cultured Chef.***

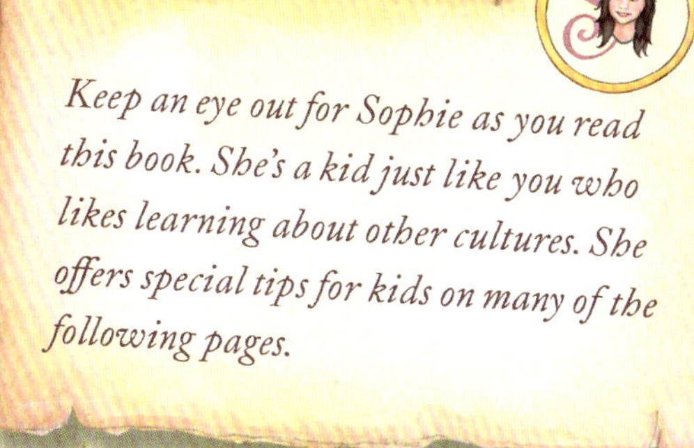

Keep an eye out for Sophie as you read this book. She's a kid just like you who likes learning about other cultures. She offers special tips for kids on many of the following pages.

As you read this book, look for phrases in other languages. A fun activity is translating these phrases using the website translate.google.com. Surprise your friends with your new language skills.

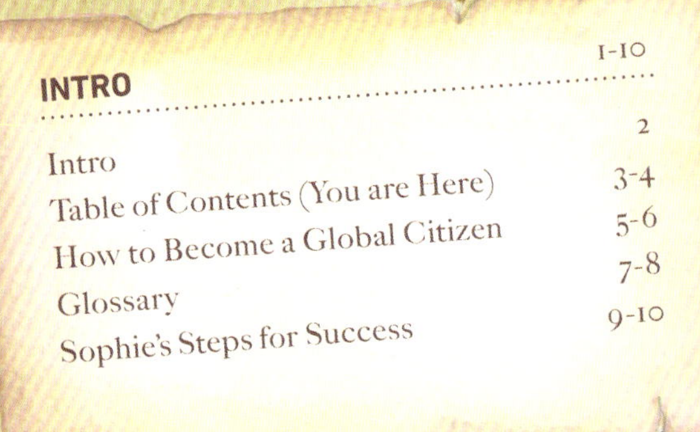

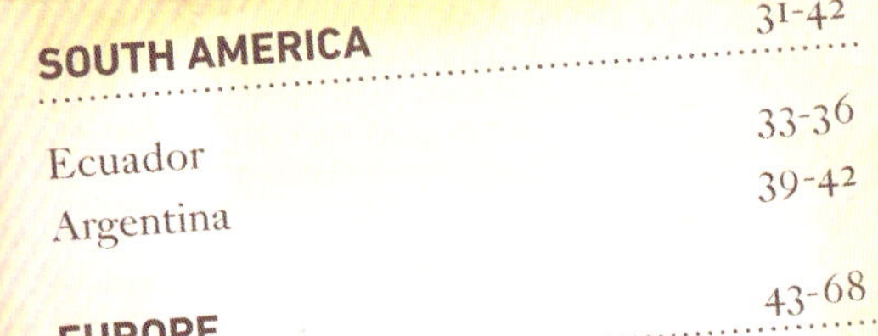

Table of Contents

HOW TO BECOME A GLOBAL CITIZEN

What does it mean to be a global citizen? We live in a world that is becoming increasingly interconnected. Through technology, improvements in international travel options and exciting communication tools, such as Google Translate and Facebook, the world is becoming a much smaller place. Now it is possible to conduct business, make new friends and help others through global philanthropy with the simple click of a mouse.

Why Become a Global Citizen?

Learning about other cultures helps you become a well-rounded person, improving your ability to communicate better, meet new friends and get a better job. The more you study about the world you'll realize there are others who may be less fortunate than you. You can find ways to improve their lives through politics, philanthropy and volunteer efforts.

5 Ways to Become More Globally Aware

1. Develop an interest in how others do things differently around the world.
2. Read books, watch movies and listen to music from or about other countries.
3. Be open to experiencing new things. Try your hand at making art, music and food like they do in other cultures.
4. Find out who is in need and how you can help. It doesn't matter whether you find the need in your own neighborhood or halfway around the world — simple things you do can make a huge difference in the lives of others.
5. Inspire future travel by learning about the culture, history and geography of places around the world.

What is Philanthropy?

Philanthropy begins when you realize that there are people in the world whose basic needs of food, clothing, shelter and education are not being met. It involves giving to an organization or individual who is actively helping to meet those needs or giving directly to the person in need. Giving can take many forms, whether you donate things you already own, your money or your time.

Here Are Some Ways You Can Start Making A Difference

Donate toys, school supplies and clothes to an orphanage or local shelter.

Make fun crafts or handmade books and deliver them to a retirement center.

Volunteer with your parents to do yard work for a senior in your neighborhood.

Volunteer at a soup kitchen or coordinate a canned food drive.

Visit Kiva.org and learn about micro-lending.

Introduce yourself to someone new at school and help make them feel special.

Hold a bake sale or carwash to raise money for someone in need.

Adopt an animal from a shelter or rescue facility.

Look for volunteer opportunities within your school, church or community.

Make ethical purchasing decisions and buy organic foods and fair trade goods whenever possible.

Learn a Foreign Language

Learning a foreign language allows us to better communicate with our friends and neighbors. High schools in the United States require students study a foreign language, but many students don't enjoy the experience. What about you? Why not try to make learning a foreign language fun? Many phrasebooks and games are available to help make learning a new language enjoyable.

GLOSSARY

Al Dente:
This is an Italian phrase that describes a way to cook pasta so it is tender but still a little firm.

Beat:
Stirring really fast so you can add air into whatever you're mixing. Beating makes your mixture lighter and fluffier.

Blend:
Completely combine ingredients until everything is all mixed up and very smooth.

Coat:
Covering a food up with a layer of another ingredient, like dipping a strawberry in chocolate.

Combine:
Stirring together two or more ingredients until they are blended.

Cut In:
Mixing the solid fat into dry ingredients until they are all the same size pieces.

De-bone:
Taking the meat off of the bones.

Dice:
Cutting into very small pieces about 1/8 to ¼ inch.

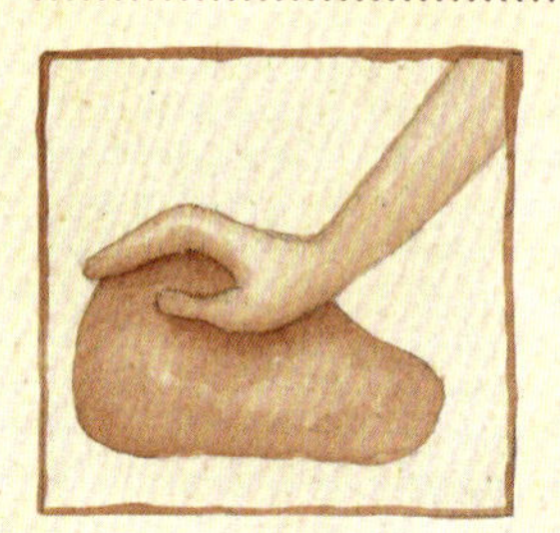

Knead:
Working the dough. Do this by folding and pressing dough together with the heels of your hands. Turn the pressed dough around by one quarter turn each time.

Marinate:
Soaking food in a sauce. Usually it is meat or vegetables. Place the food in a dish or bowl and pour the sauce over the top to cover it.

Mince:
Chopping into very fine pieces — smaller than a dice.

Mix:
Stirring until everything is blended together.

GLOSSARY

Preheat:
Turning on the oven ahead of time to make sure it is at the right temperature when it is time to cook the food.

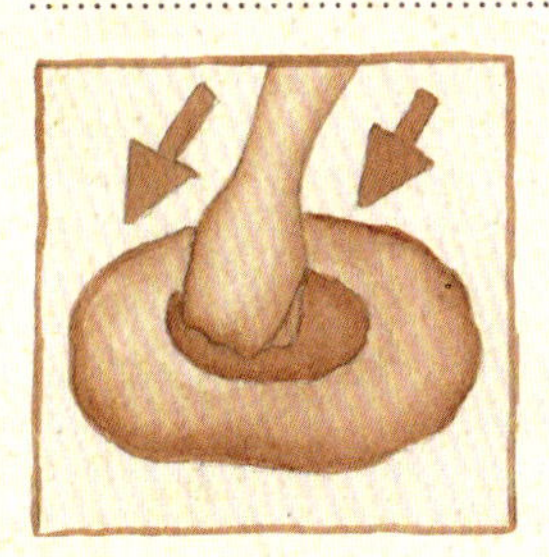

Punch-down:
Pushing down the puffed up dough with your fist. This makes the air come out, so you can work with it again.

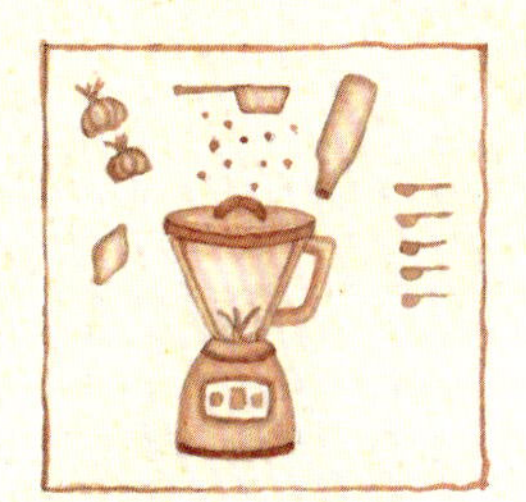

Puree:
Using a blender or a sieve to turn food into a smooth, thick mixture.

Season:
Adding spices, herbs, salt or pepper to enhance the natural flavor of food.

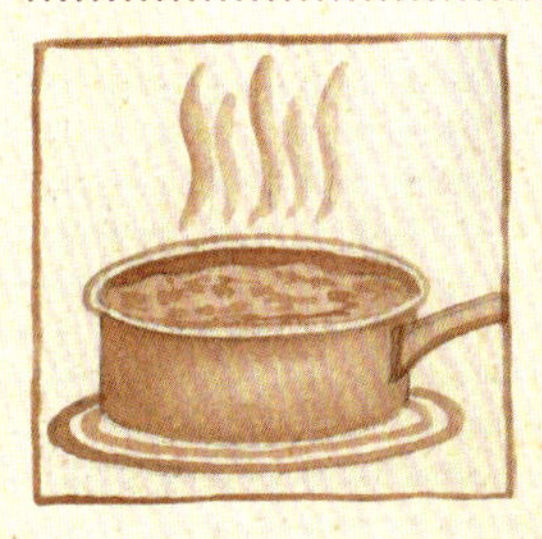

Simmer:
Cooking in liquid over low heat. It's still bubbling a little, but it's not hot enough to boil.

Skewer:
Putting small pieces of food onto a bamboo or metal stick to cook or to serve. The stick is also called a skewer.

Stir:
Mixing up ingredients with a spoon in big, slow circles so you don't beat in any air.

Tender:
Neither hard nor mushy. When something is tender, it is easy to stick a fork into it, but it doesn't fall apart when you do.

Toss:
Lifting and turning ingredients quickly with two forks or spoons.

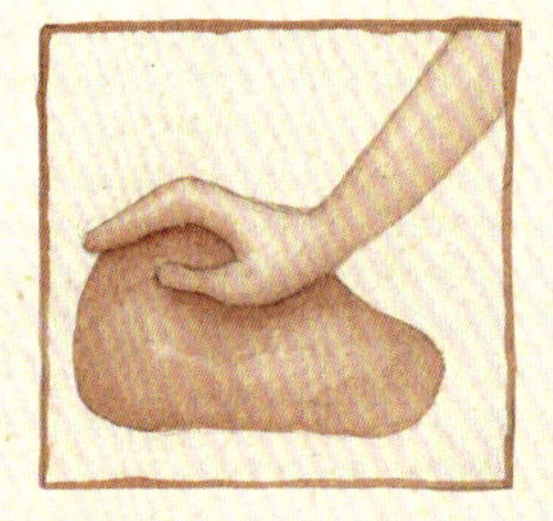

Turn-out:
Tumbling the dough out of the bowl onto a floured board or cloth so you can knead it.

Glossary Activity:
If you ever find a word in a recipe you don't understand, why not look it up in the dictionary? Soon you'll become quite the expert as you continue to add words to your cooking and baking vocabulary.

The Home Baking Association has provided a fun Memory Match game you can play to improve your kitchen vocabulary. homebaking.org/memory/memorygame.php

SOPHIE'S TEN STEPS FOR SUCCESS IN THE KITCHEN

With so many ingredients and complicated instructions, cooking can be a little confusing. But it doesn't have to be, especially if you learn a few of the basics first. This list of tips will help you be more organized, and will keep you safe as you prepare great tasting recipes in the kitchen with your friends and family.

1

Make sure you don't have anything else going on. You need to focus on cooking right now. Be sure you have plenty of time to do all the things the recipe says.

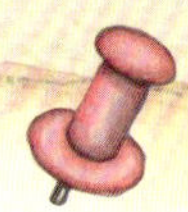

2

Read every single word of the recipe so you know all of the things you are supposed to have, both the ingredients and what kitchen tools you'll need to do the cooking. The recipe will also tell you what you are supposed to do in what order.

3

Make sure you are all cleaned up. Wash your hands really well with warm, soapy water. Dry them with a clean towel. Wear an apron and if you have long hair, put it in a ponytail.

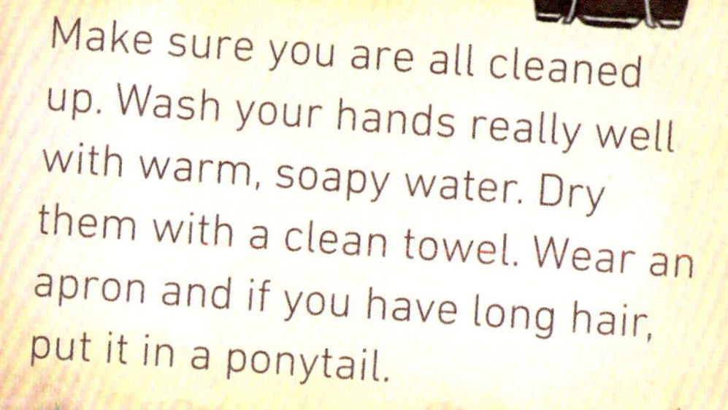

4

Keep cleaning! People are going to eat this stuff! Wipe off your counters, wash your baking dishes, measuring cups and spoons and the food you are going to cook.

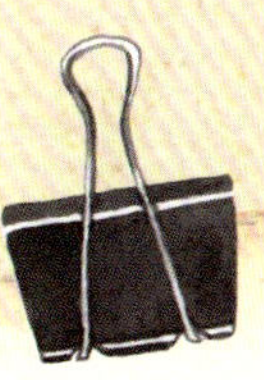

5

Set out everything you will need to make the recipe, all the ingredients and all the equipment from your kitchen.

8

Double-check the glossary to make sure you understand what all the words in the recipe mean. You want to use the right measuring cups for certain ingredients. And you want to make sure you do exactly what the recipe is telling you.

6

If you are baking something, make sure you preheat the oven before you get started. Otherwise, you're going to have to hang around and wait for the oven to get hot after everything is all put together. That might wreck the food you are trying to prepare.

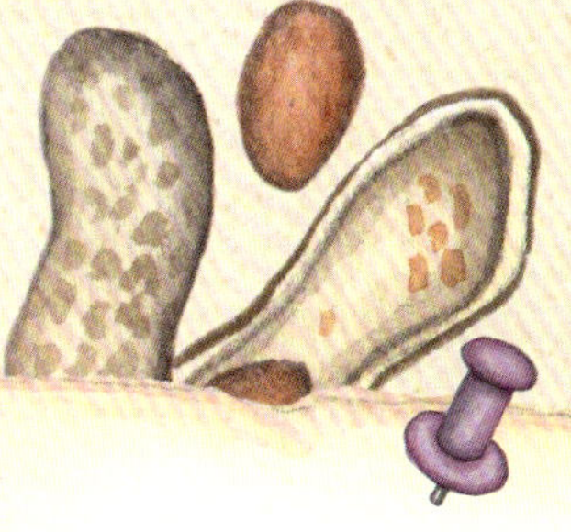

9

Be sure a grownup helps you in the kitchen. You might have to work with sharp knives and super hot ovens or burners. These are the things the adult should be doing with you or for you.

7

Measure out all of your ingredients before you start mixing it all together and cooking. Line them up on the counter leaving plenty of room for your workspace.

10

It is always a good idea to clean up as you work. If you have everything together before you start, you can stay on top of each task. Put used utensils in a sink of soapy water or in the dishwasher as you finish. It is a lot more fun to cook if you do not have to clean up a really big mess when you are all done!

"We hold these truths to be self-evident, that all men are created equal."

American President, Thomas Jefferson

"We hold these truths to be self-evident, that all men are created equal."

NORTH AMERICA
N
E
W
S
HAWAII - HAITI - MEXICO - JAMAICA

(USA) Hawaii

The Hawaiian Hula is a method of storytelling through dance and intricate hand movements. It was invented by the Polynesians who first settled the islands and has become a significant part of Hawaiian culture, performed for both religious and entertainment purposes.

Hula dancers typically wear floor-length grass skirts as well as special ornamentation such as headpieces, necklaces and bracelets. Floral garlands called lei are used in ceremonies as well, with different floral and leaf patterns each carrying its own symbolism and importance.

The art form of hula requires knowledge of the many different hand motions and gestures used to tell a story. The simplest of hand movements can signify something as complex as the birth of a child or as simple as a tree swaying in the wind.

Music is an important component of Hula, with many traditional instruments used to accompany the dance. Several instruments such as the Ipu Drum and Nose Flutes are carved from hollow reeds and gourds.

Hibiscus Flower - *Hibiscus furcellatus*

Musubi Riceballs

The people of Hawaii have a complex cultural history that begins with their Polynesian beginnings. If a Hawaiian family can trace their history back many generations, they are considered native. Throughout the history of Hawaii, its natural beauty and geographic location have attracted many different groups of people to the islands.

When sugar plantations became big business in Hawaii in the 1850s, many Asian workers relocated to the islands. Today Chinese, Japanese and Filipinos make up almost 40 percent of the island population. The multi-cultural residents have integrated customs, foods and traditions from other countries into the Hawaiian way of life.

The Japanese dish Musubi has become a favorite food in Hawaii. It is prepared with either pickled plums or small wedges of luncheon meats. The small rice balls are served as a convenient snack food wrapped with a distinctive band of nori (seaweed paper).

The tradition of May Day in Hawaii is a little different. Hawaiians give the gift of a lei accompanied by a kiss for good luck on May 1st each year.

How to Make Your Own Lei

Step 1 - Cut an appropriate length of string to hang like a necklace (16-20 inches depending on your size). Make a knot at one end of the string.

Step 2 - Create and cut 10-15 flowers from brightly colored paper. Do the same with 10-15 leaves on green paper, making sure the leaves are just a bit larger than the flowers.

Step 3 - Using a hole punch, create a small hole in the exact center of each piece.

Step 4 - Count how many flowers and leaves you have in total. Cut that many 1½-inch long pieces of drinking straws.

Step 5 - String all of your pieces on the string, creating a leaf, flower, straw pattern. Make a knot after the last piece, then tie both ends of the string together to form your very own lei.

Musubi Riceballs

STEP BY STEP

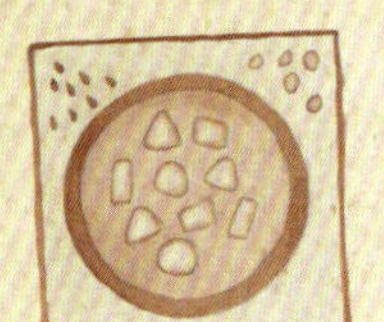

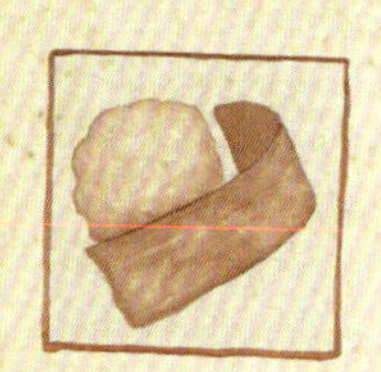

1. Soak the rice for one hour, then prepare as directed on packaging.
2. Cut two sheets of nori into nine strips about ¾-inch wide.
3. Remove the pits from the umeboshi and pat dry with a paper towel.
4. Wet your hands then mold a handful of rice into a 2-inch ball.
5. Sprinkle with sesame seeds.
6. Press a piece of umeboshi into the center
7. Place a band of nori around the outer edge of the ball.

Continue assembling the Musubi until you've exhausted your supplies. You may sprinkle each rice ball with sesame seeds or aonori if desired.

SOPHIE'S TIP FOR KIDS

"I think you should try umeboshi because it is something new and different. If you really don't like it, try pressing dried apricot or a fresh grape in the center instead."

WHAT YOU'LL NEED

INGREDIENTS

- 3 cups sticky rice (glutinous rice or sweet rice)
- 1¼ cups water
- 4 sheets nori (seaweed paper)
- 4 to 5 umeboshi (pickled plums)
- 2 teaspoons toasted sesame seeds
- Salt (to taste)

OPTIONAL INGREDIENTS

- Aonori (crushed green seaweed)
- Sesame seeds

Nutrition Facts : Serving Size: (100g) | Servings: 10

	% Daily Value
Calories: 250 — Calories From Fat 15	
Total Fat: 1.5g	2%
Saturated Fat: 0.5g	3%
Trans Fat: 0g	
Cholesterol: 0mg	0%
Sodium: 150mg	6%
Total Carbohydrate: 52g	17%
Dietary Fiber: 1g	4%
Sugars: 0g	
Protein: 7g	

HAWAII

Capital City / Honolulu

Nation Language / English, Hawaiian

Population / 1,392,313

Currency / Dollar

United States of America is comprised of fifty states, with Hawaii being the most recent addition on August 21, 1959. The state of Hawaii is actually a group of more than eight islands with the city of Honolulu as their capital.

The Hawaiian Naupaka Legend

There once was a Hawaiian maiden who lived high on the mountain. Every day she traveled down the slopes to the ocean shore where she bathed and played in the sun. One day a vibrant green honu (Hawaiian Green Sea Turtle, *Chelonia mydas*) saw the girl and became enchanted by her beauty. But the turtle was actually a kupua, a shape-shifting trickster god who could take on any appearance he liked.

Overwhelmed by his love for the girl, the kupua turned himself into a handsome young man and bodysurfed to the shore. The young man professed his love for the girl and each day when she came to the water's edge they would splash and play until sunset. The girl then returned to the mountain each night.

Disheartened by her departure every evening, the young man proposed to the girl one afternoon. Together they found a village elder and asked him to perform the marriage ceremony. But the elder realized the young man was actually a shape-shifter kupua, and consequently a marriage between the two was forbidden.

Frustrated, the kupua found a beautiful white flower blossoming on a nearby tree. He gave half of one of the blossoms to the girl and left the other half on the tree. With tears in his eyes, he told the girl if she wished to see him again, she would bring her flower to this tree and reunite it with its other half. He would then return from the ocean and they would be together again.

Green Sea Turtle - *Chelonia mydas*

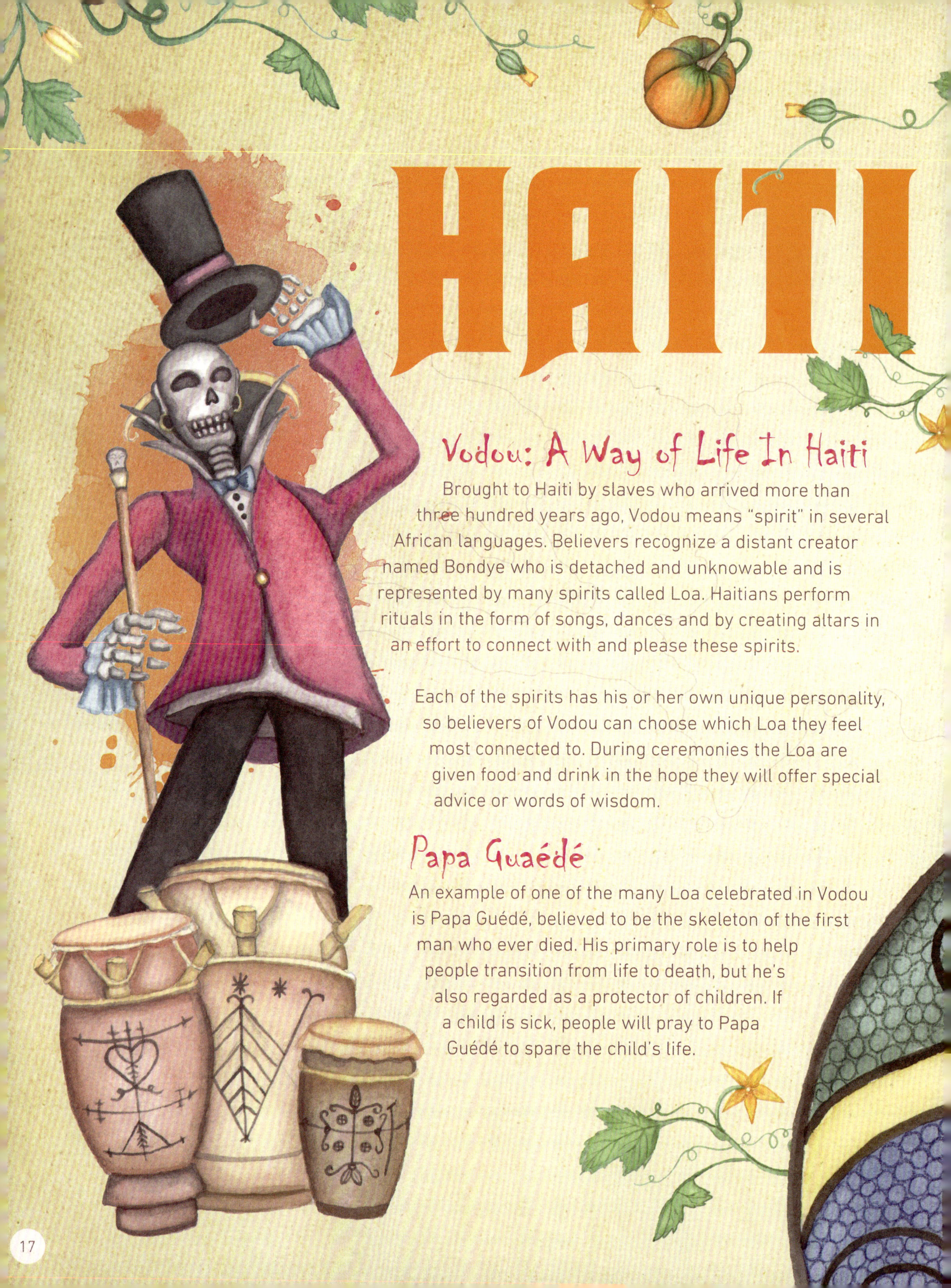

HAITI

Vodou: A Way of Life In Haiti

Brought to Haiti by slaves who arrived more than three hundred years ago, Vodou means "spirit" in several African languages. Believers recognize a distant creator named Bondye who is detached and unknowable and is represented by many spirits called Loa. Haitians perform rituals in the form of songs, dances and by creating altars in an effort to connect with and please these spirits.

Each of the spirits has his or her own unique personality, so believers of Vodou can choose which Loa they feel most connected to. During ceremonies the Loa are given food and drink in the hope they will offer special advice or words of wisdom.

Papa Guaédé

An example of one of the many Loa celebrated in Vodou is Papa Guédé, believed to be the skeleton of the first man who ever died. His primary role is to help people transition from life to death, but he's also regarded as a protector of children. If a child is sick, people will pray to Papa Guédé to spare the child's life.

Haitian Freedom Soup

For over one hundred years, the French controlled Haiti, taking advantage of the many natural resources and growing conditions the land had to offer. In order to farm massive amounts of sugar, coffee, cotton and indigo on their plantations, the French imported nearly one million slaves from Africa. Today a major percentage of Haiti's population traces their ancestry to the African slaves.

The French plantation owners treated the slaves terribly, offering them only the minimum of what they needed to survive. While the slaves dined on a thin bread soup, the plantation owners enjoyed a rich and hearty pumpkin soup. In fact, the slaves were forbidden to eat the soup because it was considered too fancy for the simple people.

After more than one hundred years, the people of Haiti were fed up with the French. They began fighting back in 1791 and after a long battle won their independence! What was one of the first things they did following their victory? They celebrated by eating pumpkin soup! To this day, pumpkin soup is served in millions of homes every year on January 1 as a reminder of Haitian independence.

Haitian Freedom Soup

STEP BY STEP

1 In a large pot, add the pumpkin and water, stirring until it reaches an even consistency.

2 Press cloves halfway into the flesh of the pepper, then add to pumpkin mixture.

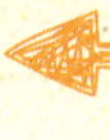

3 Add carrots, cabbage, nutmeg, lime juice and zest, salt and pepper. Cover and bring to a boil.

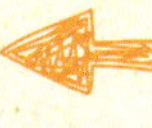

4 Reduce heat to medium-low and simmer for 10 minutes. Stir in macaroni, parsley and coconut milk, cover again and simmer gently until pasta is tender and soup is thickened, about 10 minutes more. Add more water to thin the soup if you find it too thick.

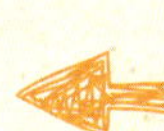

5 Be creative with your presentation. Serve with a dollop of sour cream and a sprinkle of crushed pistachios or whatever else you like.

SOPHIE'S TIP FOR KIDS

"I love making designs with pumpkin seeds on top of this soup. You can buy different flavors of roasted pumpkin seeds at the store, or you can look up instructions online on how to make your own at home."

Nutrition Facts : Serving Size: (451g) | Servings: 10

	% Daily Value
Calories: 120 — Calories From Fat 30	
Total Fat: 3.5g	5%
Saturated Fat: 3g	15%
Trans Fat: 0g	
Cholesterol: 0mg	0%
Sodium: 40mg	2%
Total Carbohydrate: 21g	7%
Dietary Fiber: 3g	12%
Sugars: 6g	
Protein: 4g	

WHAT YOU'll NEED

INGREDIENTS

2 pounds fresh pumpkin (2 cups mashed)
10 cups water, plus more if needed
1 13.5-ounce can of unsweetened coconut milk
1 jalapeño or serrano pepper
10 whole cloves
4 carrots, peeled and sliced
1/2 small head green cabbage, cored and chopped
1/2 teaspoon ground nutmeg
1 tablespoon curry powder
medium lime (zest and juice)
1/4 pound macaroni
1/4 cup chopped parsley
Salt and pepper to taste

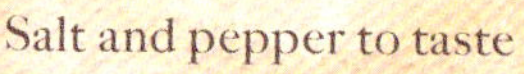

HAITI

Capital City / Port-au- Prince

Nation Language / French

Population / 9,719,932

Currency / Gourde

Haiti occupies a smaller portion of the island of Hispaniola, which it shares with the Spanish-speaking country the Dominican Republic. The name of the country is derived from the native Taíno word Ayiti, meaning "land of high mountains."

Uncle Bouki and Ti Malice: A Haitian Folktale

One fine morning, Uncle Bouki was walking down the lane when his stomach began kicking and dancing; he was very hungry! While he rushed home to prepare a meal for himself, he saw a toothless old woman eating alongside the road.

"Mmmm, that looks delicious," Uncle Bouki said. "What are you eating?" Distracted by the nosey Uncle Bouki, the old woman bit her lip and screamed out, "Ay-yai!"

With no time to lose, Uncle Bouki raced to the market in search of some delicious ay-yai for himself. The poor man was very hungry indeed! But when he arrived at the market and began asking questions, the vendors only laughed at him because ay-yai didn't exist at all!

"I'm so hungry, I can't think of anything else," Uncle Bouki said to Ti Malice when he returned home. "Do you have any ay-yai?"

Ti Malice wanted to teach silly Uncle Bouki a lesson, so he gathered a number of items and placed them in a bag. "Here's your ay-yai; it's the best I have."

Uncle Bouki pulled out an orange from the bag and said, "No, this isn't what I'm looking for." Next, he pulled out a pineapple and just shook his head. "No, not this one either." Finally, he reached into the bag and pulled out a piece of cactus.

"Ay-yai, ay-yai!" screamed Uncle Bouki as the prickly cactus spines poked into his skin. "What did you do that for?" he asked. Ti Malice couldn't control his laughter and answered, "You asked for some Ay-yai, and that's just what you got!"

SHOPPING FOR A GLOBAL KITCHEN

If you are a young cook and want a little help with some of these activities, you can ask your older brother, sister, neighbor, friend or cousin to help you out. Spending time in the kitchen is always lots of fun, no matter how old you are. If you are a teen-aged chef, consider including a younger chef in these activities as a way to enrich your own experience. You could have a lot more fun teaching or helping youngsters with their first cooking and shopping activities.

Shopping at the International Market

Do you have an international recipe in mind for dinner tonight? If you're looking for recipes that are a little outside your normal eating habits, shop at an ethnic market first for authentic spices and ingredients. Local ethnic grocery stores generally have less expensive prices than supermarkets. And you will most likely discover new foods, meet different people, and benefit your neighborhood economy by shopping locally.

Take your cookbook or your recipes with you. Ask questions about the food and other products at the store. The store clerk will probably have lots of ideas about your recipes and how to help make it very authentic or give it a personal "twist." Plus you could learn a lot of cool things about cultures & cooking!

Shopping at the International Market

"Can you tell me what this ingredient is?"

"What does it taste like?"

"How do you use it?"

"Have you ever made a recipe like this before?"

"How do you pronounce this?"

"Do you have any ideas to help me make this recipe more like something you might make?"

"What is it?"

Visit Your Local Farmer's Market

Visit your local farmers' marketplace. Sure, the farmers in your market are from your own region, but that is exactly what makes it like going to an open-air market or bazaar to pick up your weekly food items. Ours is one of the very few cultures that has large grocery stores where you can purchase everything you need for your home during any given week. The fact is: most other countries have marketplaces where vendors work from stalls every day just like our local farmers do on weekends. We think it's entertainment, but for everyone else around the world, it's a way of life.

THE INTERNATIONAL PANTRY

When you decide that you want to try to cook some of the foods that your friends from other countries have grown up eating, you will need to have a few of the ingredients from those cultures and recipes on hand in your kitchen.

Because our American culture is becoming more globally aware all the time, a lot of the ingredients in the recipes of this cookbook can be found at your neighborhood grocery store. Even though these ingredients are organized by the cultures in this section, lots of foods, spices, and herbs are used across many different cultures.

MEXICO

DAY OF THE DEAD

If you were to imagine Halloween and Memorial Day combined, how do you think the celebration would go? Chances are it would look a lot like Dia de Los Muertos (Day of the Dead). The Mexican holiday honors those who have died with a national fiesta complete with food, music, flowers and art.

Catrina

Day of the Dead wouldn't be complete without the Catrina, created by artist Jose Guadalupe Posada in the early 1900s. She is a fancy skeleton lady dressed in expensive dresses with big scarves and floppy hats. She was designed to remind the people that everyone faces death similarly, whether they are rich or poor.

Frida

Catrina in Mexican folk art may take many forms. For example, the Catrina represented on the left side of this page is in the style of artist Frida Kahlo. Kahlo began painting after a terrible bus accident left her severely injured. During her life, she spent countless hours confined to her bed where she painted self-portraits to pass the time. Today, some of those self-portraits have gone on to sell for more than a million dollars.

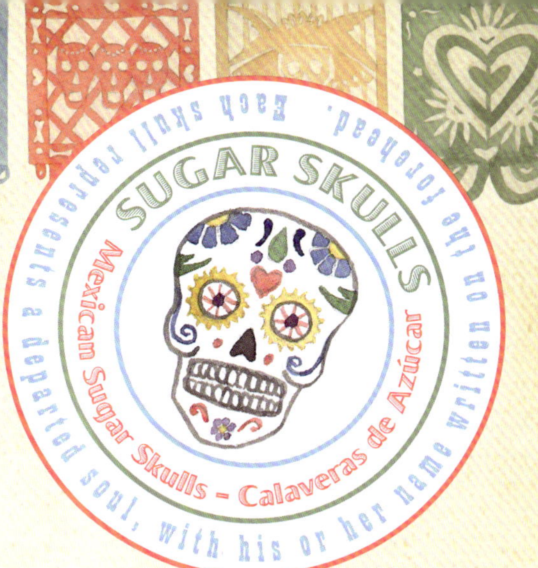

SUGAR SKULLS
Mexican Sugar Skulls - Calaveras de Azúcar
Each skull represents a departed soul, with his or her name written on the forehead.

Monarch Butterfly - *Danaus plexippus*

Day of the Dead Bread

(Pan de Muerte)

Every year on the evening of November 1, cemeteries all over Mexico are filled to the brim with families celebrating their loved ones who have passed away. Complete with music and food, the celebration feels more like a birthday party than a funeral. It often lasts until the early morning hours with plenty to eat and drink. Bread and Day of the Dead go hand-in-hand.

Bakeries on every street corner sell the sweet, round bread in the days leading up to November 1. Loaves are available in many different sizes and often have small decorations baked into them in the shape of tear drops, hearts, flowers and bones. These rolls are placed with the flowers and decorations until they are eaten in the morning when families prepare to return home.

Some Like It Hot: *If there is one vegetable that best represents Mexican cuisine, it is the chili pepper. What kind of peppers do you like? Research the different varieties of peppers available, and, if you can take the heat, try one or two the next time you're at the market.*

Bread of the Dead

STEP BY STEP

1. In a medium saucepan, heat the milk and butter together until the butter melts completely. Remove the mixture from the heat and add 1/4 cup warm water (it should be around 110 degrees Fahrenheit).

2. In a large bowl, combine the all-purpose flour, yeast, salt, anise seed and sugar. Beat in the warm milk mixture, then add eggs and orange zest and beat until well combined. Stir in ½ cup of flour, then continue adding more flour until the dough is soft.

3. Turn the dough out onto a lightly floured surface and knead until smooth and elastic.

4. Place the dough in a lightly greased bowl, cover with plastic wrap and let rise in a warm place until doubled in size. This will take about one to two hours. Punch the dough down and shape it into a large round loaf. Place dough onto a baking sheet, loosely cover with plastic wrap and let rise in a warm place for about one hour or until nearly doubled in size.

5. Bake in a preheated 350 degree Fahrenheit oven for about 35 to 45 minutes. Remove from the oven, let cool slightly then brush with glaze.

6. To make the glaze: In a small saucepan combine sugar, orange juice and orange zest. Bring to a boil over medium heat and boil for two minutes. Brush over the top of bread while still warm. Sprinkle glazed bread with white sugar.

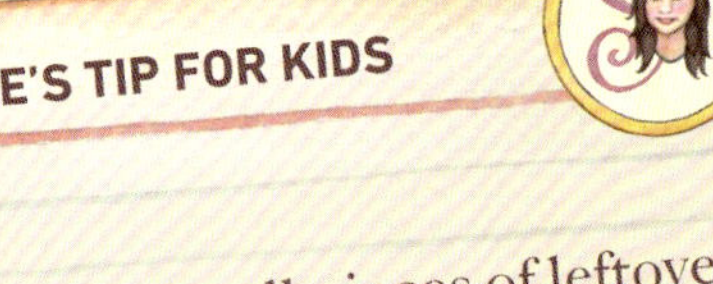

SOPHIE'S TIP FOR KIDS

"I like using small pieces of leftover dough to make designs on top of my loaves before they go in the oven. You can make bones, rays of a sun or anything else you can imagine!"

Nutrition Facts : Serving Size: (69g) | Servings: 12

	% Daily Value
Calories: 200	Calories From Fat 45
Total Fat: 5g	8%
Saturated Fat: 3g	15%
Trans Fat: 0g	
Cholesterol: 40mg	13%
Sodium: 115mg	5%
Total Carbohydrate: 34g	11%
Dietary Fiber: 1g	4%
Sugars: 9g	
Protein: 5g	

WHAT YOU'LL NEED

INGREDIENTS

- 1/4 cup unsalted butter
- 1/4 cup milk
- 1/4 cup warm water
- 3 cups all-purpose flour
- 1 1/4 teaspoons active dry yeast
- 1/2 teaspoon salt
- 2 teaspoons anise seed
- 1/4 cup sugar
- 2 large eggs, beaten
- 2 teaspoon orange zest

INGREDIENTS - GLAZE

- 1/4 cup sugar
- 1/4 cup orange juice
- 1 tablespoon orange zest

MEXICO

Capital City / Mexico City

Nation Language / Spanish

Population / 117,409,830

Currency / Peso

Mexico is the site of several ancient civilizations including the Olmec, Toltec, Zapotec, Mayan and Aztec peoples. Each civilization has made an impact on the culture and traditions of the country.

Marigold – Tagetes erecta

What is an Altar?

Altars (Ofrenda) offer a way for people to remember their loved ones who have passed away. Although most altars are in private homes, many are on display publicly in the community as well.

An altar represents the four elements of nature: Earth, Wind, Water and Fire. Here's a brief overview of each of those elements.

Earth - is represented by agricultural elements like fruit or vegetables. The aroma of the food gives the dead an opportunity to replenish their energy after their long journey home.

Wind - is represented by objects that flutter in the breeze like colorful paper cutouts called papel picado or bundles of wheat or corn.

Water - is always available for the departed in either a pitcher with glasses or a bottle. Water also signifies purity and renewal.

Fire - is represented in altars by candles of all shapes and sizes. The flames help to attract spirits who might have lost their way.

The Mexican Marigold

Marigold flowers are known in Mexico as Cempasúchil and are often referred to as the Flower of the Dead. They are used extensively in altars because it is believed their strong odor and bright color help guide the spirits home.

Do It Yourself: Plant your own marigold flowers at home this spring! Whether you are looking for flowers big or small, marigolds provide blooms all summer long.

JAMAICA

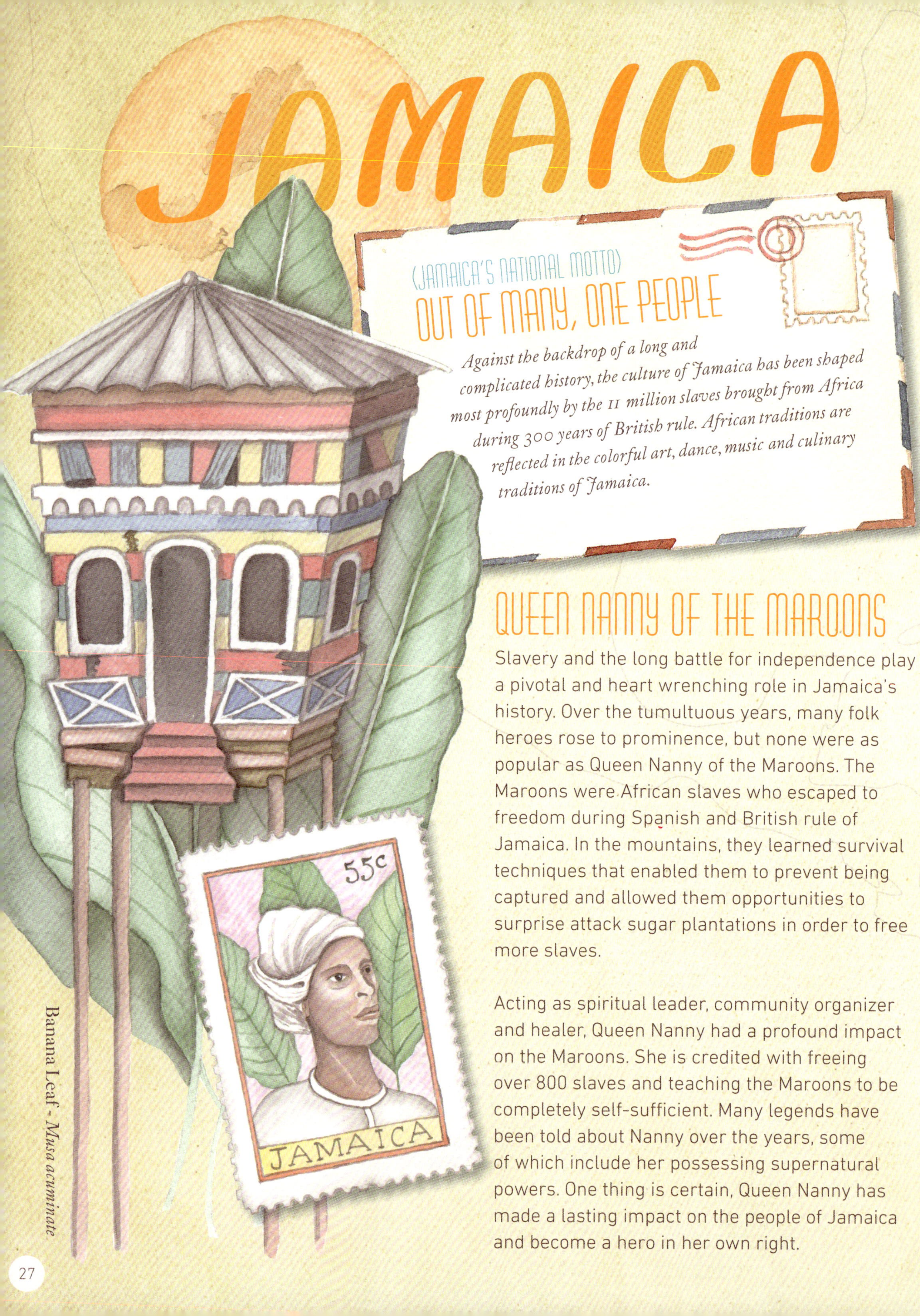

Banana Leaf - *Musa acuminate*

(JAMAICA'S NATIONAL MOTTO)

OUT OF MANY, ONE PEOPLE

Against the backdrop of a long and complicated history, the culture of Jamaica has been shaped most profoundly by the 11 million slaves brought from Africa during 300 years of British rule. African traditions are reflected in the colorful art, dance, music and culinary traditions of Jamaica.

QUEEN NANNY OF THE MAROONS

Slavery and the long battle for independence play a pivotal and heart wrenching role in Jamaica's history. Over the tumultuous years, many folk heroes rose to prominence, but none were as popular as Queen Nanny of the Maroons. The Maroons were African slaves who escaped to freedom during Spanish and British rule of Jamaica. In the mountains, they learned survival techniques that enabled them to prevent being captured and allowed them opportunities to surprise attack sugar plantations in order to free more slaves.

Acting as spiritual leader, community organizer and healer, Queen Nanny had a profound impact on the Maroons. She is credited with freeing over 800 slaves and teaching the Maroons to be completely self-sufficient. Many legends have been told about Nanny over the years, some of which include her possessing supernatural powers. One thing is certain, Queen Nanny has made a lasting impact on the people of Jamaica and become a hero in her own right.

SHRIMP JERK SKEWERS

We don't often hear the word "jerk" associated with food in the United States, but in Jamaica it has been for many years. Jerk is a style of cooking in which meat is either rubbed or marinated in a blend of spices before cooking. And we're not talking about a couple spices here — traditional jerk seasoning recipes include 15-20 ingredients for a mouth-wateringly complex combination of flavors!

We're using shrimp in this recipe because the Jamaicans have a special place in their hearts for this shellfish. In a region called the Middle Quarters, Jamaican street food vendors line the streets selling plastic bags of bright red shrimp to locals and tourists alike. Wearing white aprons and cooking over hissing grills and bubbling pots, the cooks call out and wave their bags of shrimp to passing cars and trucks all day long.

Shrimp - *Pandalus borealis: are small free-swimming crustaceans (the same family as crabs and lobsters) that are harvested worldwide as a food source.*

The story of sugar cane and Jamaica go hand in hand. For over 150 years, millions of African slaves were transported to Jamaica to aid in the cultivation of sugar cane. The plant represents millions of dollars earned for farmers and continues to be an important crop for Jamaica today.

SHRIMP JERK SKEWERS

STEP BY STEP

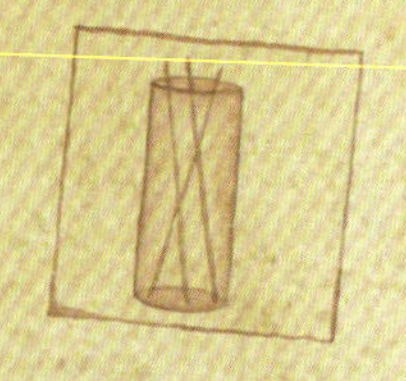

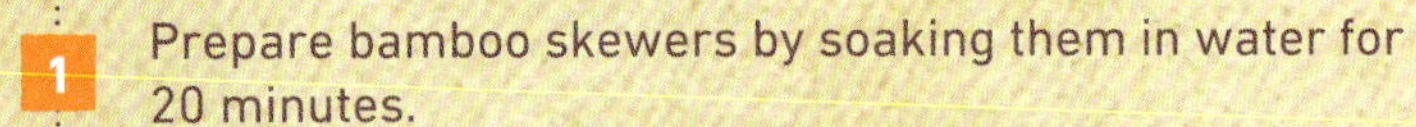

1. Prepare bamboo skewers by soaking them in water for 20 minutes.

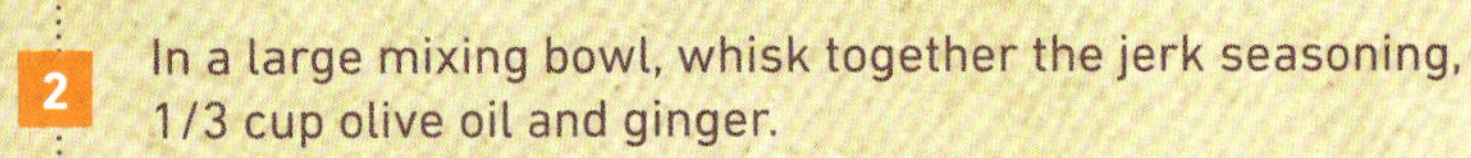

2. In a large mixing bowl, whisk together the jerk seasoning, 1/3 cup olive oil and ginger.

3. Add shrimp and pineapple to the mixture and evenly coat. Cover and let marinate for 15 minutes.

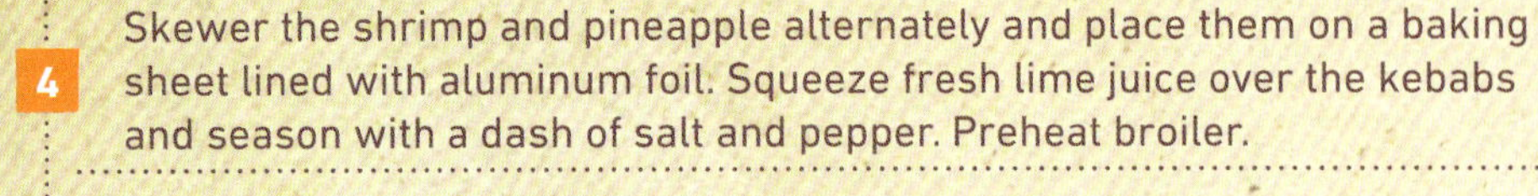

4. Skewer the shrimp and pineapple alternately and place them on a baking sheet lined with aluminum foil. Squeeze fresh lime juice over the kebabs and season with a dash of salt and pepper. Preheat broiler.

5. Cook until the pineapple is tender and the shrimp are opaque, turning the skewers once during the process (about 4-5 minutes per side).

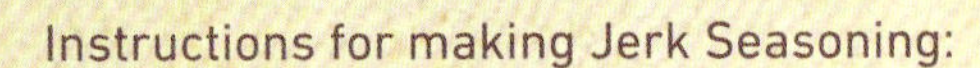

Instructions for making Jerk Seasoning:

Combine the following:

- 1 tablespoon salt
- 1 teaspoon ground allspice
- 2 teaspoons brown sugar
- 1 teaspoon garlic powder
- 1 teaspoon onion powder
- ½ teaspoon paprika
- ½ teaspoon ground nutmeg
- ½ teaspoon black pepper
- ½ teaspoon ground ginger
- ¼ teaspoon ground cinnamon
- ¼ teaspoon ground cloves
- ¼ teaspoon dried thyme
- ¼ teaspoon red pepper flakes

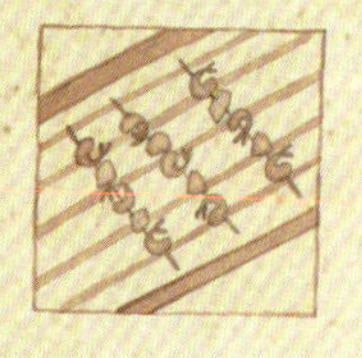

When ready to prepare your dish, use dry or mix to desired consistency using olive oil.

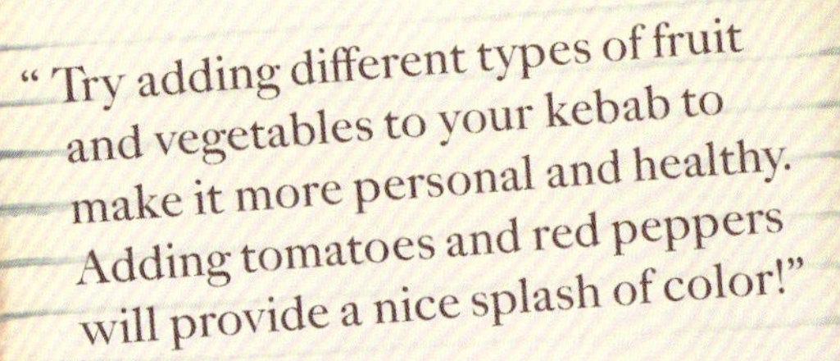

FROM THE AUTHOR

"Try adding different types of fruit and vegetables to your kebab to make it more personal and healthy. Adding tomatoes and red peppers will provide a nice splash of color!"

Nutrition Facts : Serving Size: (117g) | Servings: 8

	% Daily Value
Calories: 140 — Calories From Fat 90	
Total Fat: 10g	15%
Saturated Fat: 1.5g	8%
Trans Fat: 0g	
Cholesterol: 70mg	23%
Sodium: 320mg	13%
Total Carbohydrate: 7g	2%
Dietary Fiber: 0g	0%
Sugars: 5g	
Protein: 8g	

INGREDIENTS

Jamaican Jerk Seasoning (either prepared or using recipe provided)
1/3 cup olive oil
1½ teaspoons finely chopped ginger
1 pound large shrimp, peeled and deveined
12 pieces fresh pineapple, cut into 1-inch squares
Salt and freshly ground pepper
½ lime
Parsley for garnish

JAMAICA

Capital City / Kingston

Nation Language / English

Population / 2,88,187

Currency / Jamaican Dollar

Jamaica is "the fairest island that eyes have beheld," Christopher Columbus exclaimed when he became the first European to visit the island in 1494. The native population thought so as well when they named their island Xaymaca, meaning "the land of wood and water."

Queen Conch - *Lobatus gigas*

ANANCY: THE JAMAICAN SPIDER MAN

Always very clever, Anancy the spider man decided to collect all of the wisdom of the world to keep it safe. He looked for wisdom in all the places he'd left it, and when he was happy with what he'd found, he safely tucked it into a big cauldron with a tight lid. At first, he was pleased with his work, but soon Anancy began to have doubts. "What if someone finds the cauldron and keeps all the wisdom for himself?" he thought. So the crafty spider began looking for a new place to hide all the wisdom of the world.

Finding himself in front of a very large tamarind tree, Anancy decided he'd found the perfect hiding spot. He began pushing his heavy load up the tree but found the weight of the cauldron was too great. Happening upon this scene, Anancy's son cried out, "Father, what are you doing? If you want to carry the cauldron up the tree, you should tie it behind you. That way you can grip the tree!"

Frustrated he didn't come up with the idea himself, Anancy threw his legs up in disgrace accidentally letting the cauldron crash to the ground. With that, all the wisdom of the world tumbled into a nearby stream where it was eventually carried to the four corners of the earth. Because of Anancy's carelessness, now there is a little bit of wisdom for everybody!

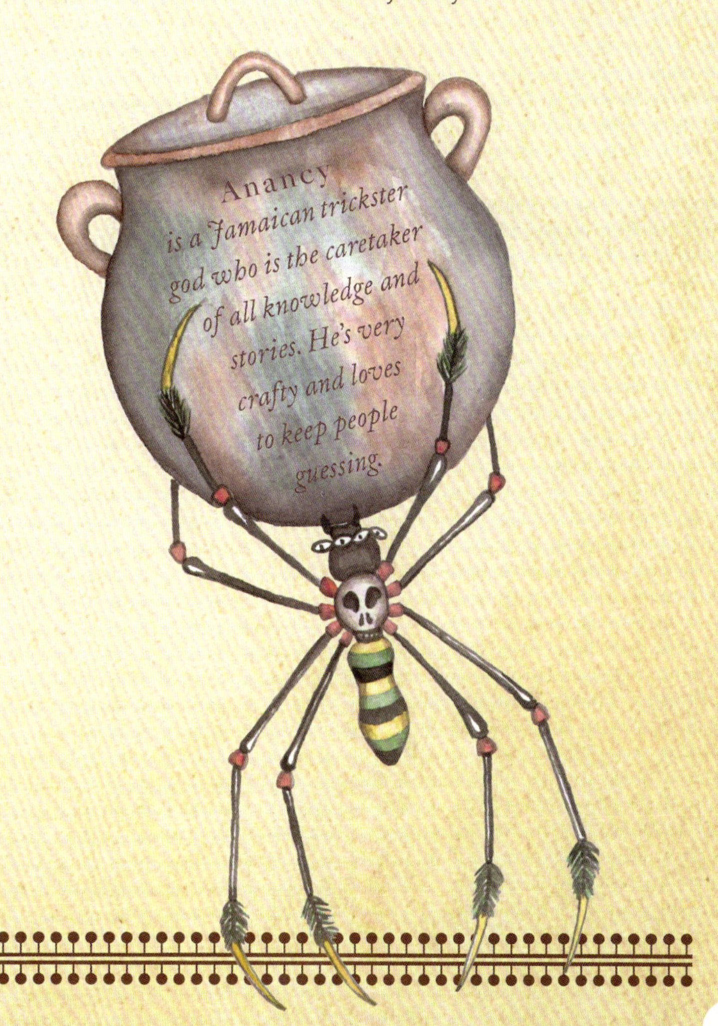
Anancy
is a Jamaican trickster
god who is the caretaker
of all knowledge and
stories. He's very
crafty and loves
to keep people
guessing.

"Shadows cannot see themselves in the mirror of the sun."

"Shadows cannot see themselves in the mirror of the sun."

First Lady of Argentina, Eva Perón

SOUTH AMERICA
N
E
W
S
ECUADOR - ARGENTINA

ECUADOR

Charles Darwin & the Voyage of the Beagle

In September 1835, a 22-year-old British naturalist named Charles Darwin spent five weeks in the Galápagos charting the geology of the islands. He didn't realize it at the time, but the observations he made and the specimens he collected during those weeks would change science forever. He eventually became one of the most famous naturalists in the world due in part to his theories on natural selection introduced in his book "On the Origin of the Species", published in 1859.

The Magnificent Galápagos Islands

The Galápagos Islands are located in the Pacific Ocean six hundred miles west of Ecuador. Constant undersea volcanic activity created this group of islands (archipelago) comprised of 14 large islands and many smaller ones. Throughout the history of the region, every time a volcano erupted, mounds of lava hardened and grew higher and higher until an island was formed. Some of the islands are still growing!

The Galápagos Islands experience pleasant weather, plenty of food and nutrients, and limited exposure to predators and humans. These special circumstances have allowed the diverse plant and animal species in the region to flourish for thousands of years. In fact, a number of these species are not found anywhere else in the world.

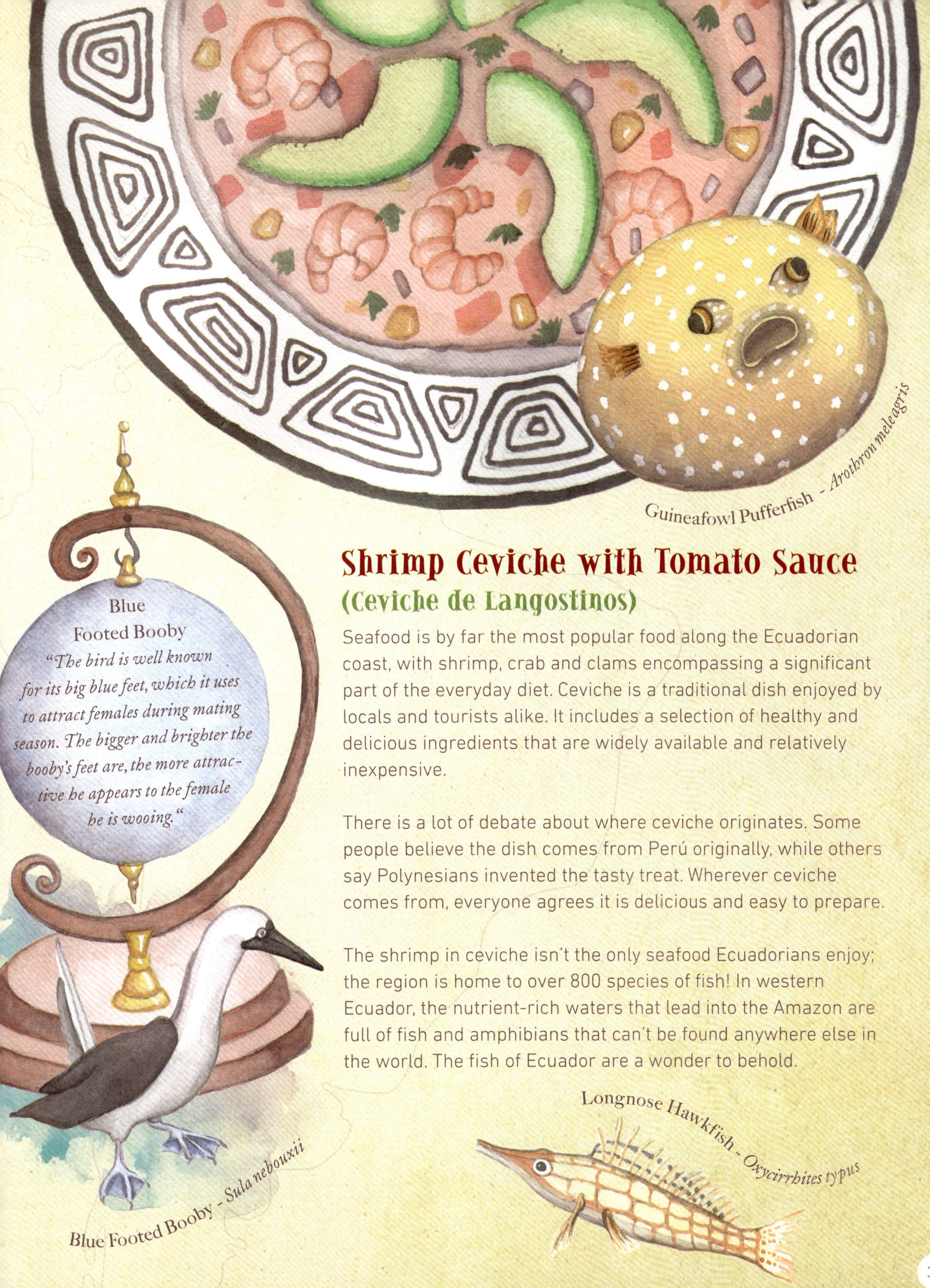

Guineafowl Pufferfish - Arothron meleagris
Blue
Footed Booby
"The bird is well known for its big blue feet, which it uses to attract females during mating season. The bigger and brighter the booby's feet are, the more attractive he appears to the female he is wooing."
Blue Footed Booby - Sula nebouxii
Longnose Hawkfish - Oxycirrhites typus

Shrimp Ceviche with Tomato Sauce

(Ceviche de Langostinos)

Seafood is by far the most popular food along the Ecuadorian coast, with shrimp, crab and clams encompassing a significant part of the everyday diet. Ceviche is a traditional dish enjoyed by locals and tourists alike. It includes a selection of healthy and delicious ingredients that are widely available and relatively inexpensive.

There is a lot of debate about where ceviche originates. Some people believe the dish comes from Perú originally, while others say Polynesians invented the tasty treat. Wherever ceviche comes from, everyone agrees it is delicious and easy to prepare.

The shrimp in ceviche isn't the only seafood Ecuadorians enjoy; the region is home to over 800 species of fish! In western Ecuador, the nutrient-rich waters that lead into the Amazon are full of fish and amphibians that can't be found anywhere else in the world. The fish of Ecuador are a wonder to behold.

Shrimp Ceviche with Tomato Sauce

STEP BY STEP

1. Dice the onion into the thinnest and smallest possible pieces.

2. Place the onion pieces in a bowl of cold, salted water and soak for 20 minutes.

3. Rinse shrimp with cold water and set aside.

4. Drain onions and rinse with cold water. Combine onions and corn with the shrimp.

5. In a small bowl, whisk together lime juice, orange juice, ketchup, sugar and vinegar. Toss with shrimp, corn, cilantro and onions. Allow the seafood to "cook" in the acidic liquid until it is opaque. Season to taste with salt and pepper.

SOPHIE'S TIP FOR KIDS

"Have you ever tried serving ceviche in a hollowed out avocado? It's delicious! Remove the pit from an avocado as well as a little bit of the meat. Replace that area with a nice scoop of ceviche."

WHAT YOU'LL NEED

INGREDIENTS

- 2-3 cups of bay shrimp
- ½ medium red onion, minced
- Juice of 1 regular lime
- ¼ cup of fresh squeezed orange juice
- ½ cup ketchup
- 1 tablespoon white vinegar
- 1 tablespoon white sugar
- 1 cup of canned corn, drained
- ½ cup of packed cilantro leaves

Juvenile King Angelfish - *Holacanthus passer*

Nutrition Facts : Serving Size: (188g) | Servings: 6

	% Daily Value
Calories: 150 — Calories From Fat 5	
Total Fat: 0g	0%
Saturated Fat: 0g	0%
Trans Fat: 0g	
Cholesterol: 230mg	77%
Sodium: 1550mg	65%
Total Carbohydrate: 14g	5%
Dietary Fiber: 0g	0%
Sugars: 8g	
Protein: 21g	

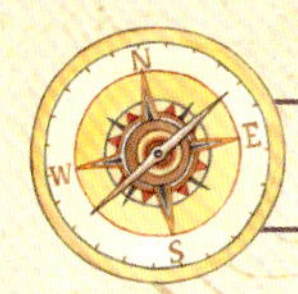

ECUADOR

Capital City / Quito

Nation Language / Spanish

Population / 15,223,680

Currency / Dollar

Ecuador is the Spanish word for equator; a name aptly given to the country situated directly in on The Equator, an imaginary line that divides the Northern and Southern hemispheres, essentially dividing the earth in half.

The Children of the Sun: The Incan Empire

Many years ago a small tribe of natives built a city named Cuzco in what is now known as Peru. The Incas were a peaceful tribe who worshipped the sun god Inti and believed their leader was the child of the sun.

In 1438 their simple way of life was threatened when a neighboring tribe called the Chancay unsuccessfully tried to conquer them. Little did the Incas know that this battle would be the impetus to them becoming a great and mighty empire!

Over the next 100 years, the Incas conquered neighboring tribes until their empire stretched over an area 2,500 miles long and 500 miles wide. Their kingdom included much of what is now known as Ecuador, and their little tribe swelled to include more than 12 million people.

As mighty as the Incas were, the arrival of Spanish invaders and a massive epidemic of smallpox devastated them. In just a few short years, between 60 to 90 percent of the Incan population was destroyed.

MUSICAL INSTRUMENTS OF THE WORLD

Can you even imagine a world without music? Consider all of the ways music has shaped your life. Do you remember your mother and father singing lullabies to you as a young child? Did you ever make up little songs to help you better learn lessons in school? Did you pass the time on long car rides with music? These are just some of the simple, everyday examples of how music impacts our lives.

Sompoton: From Northeastern Borneo, this gourd and pipe instrument is still played by the Kadasan and Dusun people. The instrument can be played in any number of orientations and can range anywhere from 6 inches to 3 feet in length. Do you think you can make your own homemade version of this instrument? Each pipe is fitted with a bamboo reed then placed in exact formation to create two rows of four pipes each, producing a complex and beautiful sound.

Marimba: Configured much in the same way as a xylophone, the marimba is a large instrument with hollowed out wooden bars that produce various tones when struck with mallets. While many cultures now include the marimba as part of their traditional music, the instrument as we know it today originates from the Garifuna people of Guatemala.

Bagpipes: The bagpipes have become such an important part of Scottish culture, it is impossible to think of the country without considering this unique instrument. But, did you know that the bagpipes didn't originate in Scotland? It is believed goat and sheep herdsmen in Samaria first made music out of animal skin and reed pipes. In fact, there are mentions of instruments resembling the bagpipes in the Old Testament of the Bible.

Accordian: A traditional instrument of folk music, the accordion has become a worldwide phenomenon that has even found its way into mainstream pop music. For thousands of years, there have been many instruments manufactured using the basic principles of the accordion, but it is believed the instrument we recognize today was created by the German instrument maker Christian Friedrich Ludwig Buschmann in 1822.

Chau Gong: Dating back to the Chinese Han Dynasty around 200 BC, the chau gong has been used for centuries to announce the presence of important officials or political figures. Typically suspended from a sturdy frame and ranging from 7 to 80 inches in diameter, the gong is struck with a mallet to produce a rich tone. These ancient musical instruments are mostly used in symphony orchestras today.

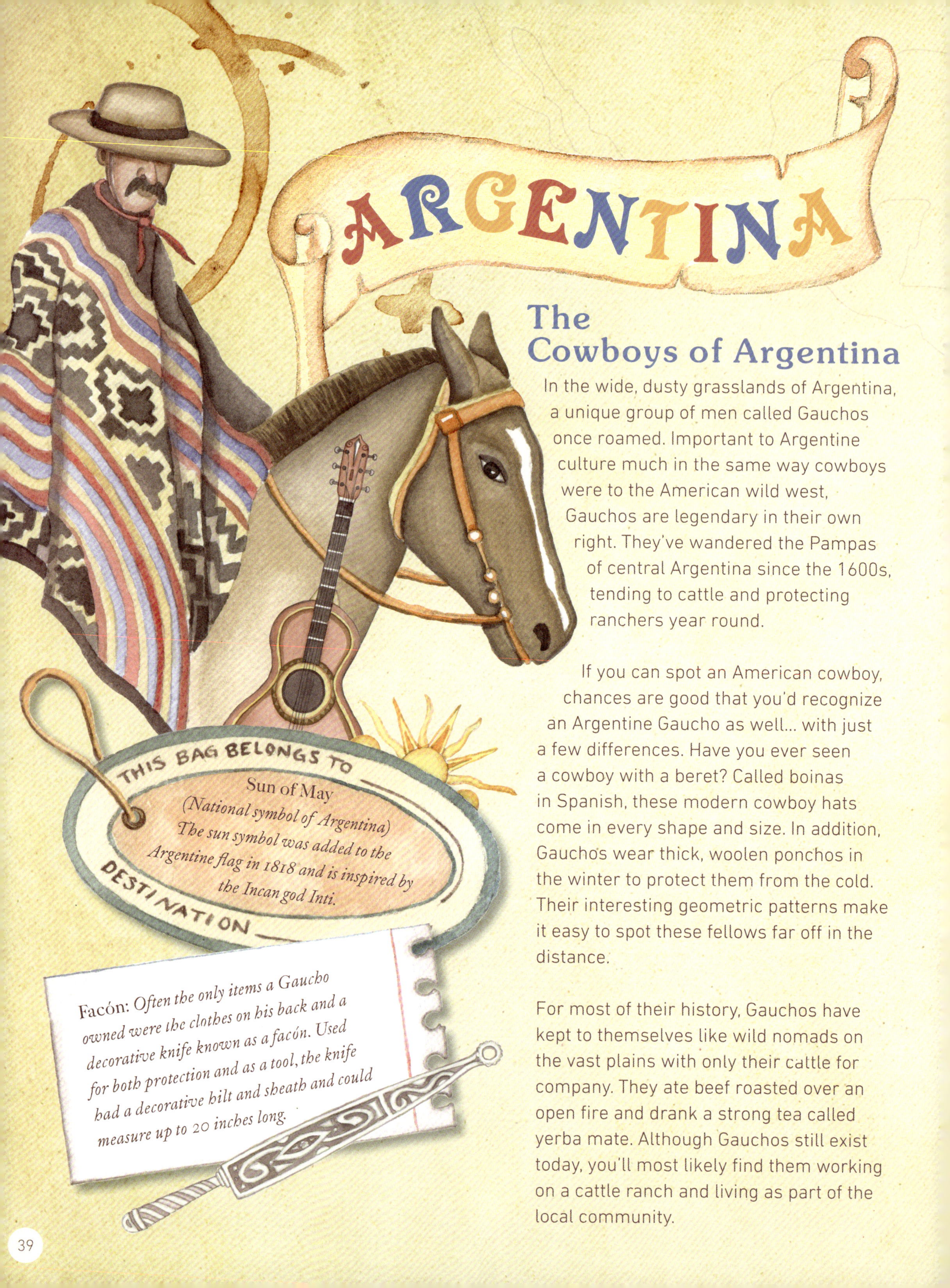

ARGENTINA
THIS BAG BELONGS TO
Sun of May
(National symbol of Argentina)
The sun symbol was added to the Argentine flag in 1818 and is inspired by the Incan god Inti.
DESTINATION
Facón: Often the only items a Gaucho owned were the clothes on his back and a decorative knife known as a facón. Used for both protection and as a tool, the knife had a decorative hilt and sheath and could measure up to 20 inches long.

The Cowboys of Argentina

In the wide, dusty grasslands of Argentina, a unique group of men called Gauchos once roamed. Important to Argentine culture much in the same way cowboys were to the American wild west, Gauchos are legendary in their own right. They've wandered the Pampas of central Argentina since the 1600s, tending to cattle and protecting ranchers year round.

If you can spot an American cowboy, chances are good that you'd recognize an Argentine Gaucho as well... with just a few differences. Have you ever seen a cowboy with a beret? Called boinas in Spanish, these modern cowboy hats come in every shape and size. In addition, Gauchos wear thick, woolen ponchos in the winter to protect them from the cold. Their interesting geometric patterns make it easy to spot these fellows far off in the distance.

For most of their history, Gauchos have kept to themselves like wild nomads on the vast plains with only their cattle for company. They ate beef roasted over an open fire and drank a strong tea called yerba mate. Although Gauchos still exist today, you'll most likely find them working on a cattle ranch and living as part of the local community.

Payada: *When Gauchos weren't tending the cattle, they could often be heard performing Payadas. A form of poetic dueling accompanied by guitar, performers would sing with partners in a question and answer format. These duels could last for many hours until they simply couldn't sing any more.*

Steak Chimichurri Pasta

The Spanish Conquistadors are responsible for introducing cattle to Argentina when they were brought over by boat in the early 1500s. Because of the country's perfect environment for raising cattle, beef production in Argentina has become a massive business and a part of the national identity. While many foods might represent Argentine culture, beef is at the top of the list.

Italian Argentinians

There are more than 24 million Italians living in Argentina, comprising over 44 percent of the immigrant population. Between the 1850s and 1940s, many Italians immigrated to Argentina because of poverty, World Wars I and II and the Great Depression. This explains why Italian culture is so prominent in the country, with pizza, pasta and gelato being some of the country's favorite dishes.

Eva Perón: *(First Lady of Argentina) 1919-1952 Eva Perón was the spiritual leader of the nation of Argentina and the wife of President Juan Perón. Although she was only 33-years-old when she died, she is remembered as one of the most fascinating women in Argentina's history.*

Boleadoras: *Used much in the same manner as a lasso, boleadoras are portions of rope with two ball weights that are used to catch animals such as sheep and cattle.*

Steak Chimichurri Pasta

STEP BY STEP

1 Place all of the chimichurri ingredients in a blender and pulse until all of the large chunks of garlic and parsley are blended nicely.

2 Prepare the steak to your desired level of doneness (stovetop, oven or grill) and set aside for 5 minutes to cool.

3 Lay the asparagus spears in a large skillet filled with 1 inch of water. Bring the water to a simmer, cover and cook for 3 to 5 minutes or until crisp-tender.

4 While the asparagus is simmering, bring a large pot of water to boil over high heat. Add bowtie pasta and cook until al dente (the noodle retaining a bit of its firmness). Drain the noodles and return to the pot.

5 Slice the steak and asparagus into 1-2-inch bite-size pieces. Toss the pasta, chimichurri, steak and asparagus together in the pot. Season with salt and pepper and additional olive oil to taste.

SOPHIE'S TIP FOR KIDS

"In Argentina many food items can be ordered *a caballo* which essentially means horseback. Whether you order pizza, pasta or bread, a caballo signifies you'd like a fried egg on top of your meal!"

Nutrition Facts : Serving Size: (264g) | Servings: 6

	% Daily Value
Calories: 560 — Calories From Fat 210	
Total Fat: 24g	37%
Saturated Fat: 4.5g	23%
Trans Fat: 0g	
Cholesterol: 45mg	15%
Sodium: 440mg	18%
Total Carbohydrate: 61g	20%
Dietary Fiber: 4g	16%
Sugars: 5g	
Protein: 29g	

INGREDIENTS - CHIMICHURRI

- 2 cloves garlic
- 1 cup Italian parsley
- 1/2 cup olive oil
- 1 teaspoon red wine vinegar
- 2 tablespoons lemon juice
- 1/2 teaspoon red pepper flakes
- 1 teaspoon salt

OTHER INGREDIENTS

- 16 ounces bowtie pasta
- 16 ounces flank steak
- 16 ounces thin asparagus

ARGENTINA

Capital City / Buenos Aires

Nation Language / Spanish

Population / 41,660,417

Currency / Peso

Argentina is the eighth largest country in the world, with more than one million square miles of land in South America. Argentina is 2,300 miles long from its border with Bolivia in the north to Isla Navarino in the south.

The Mythical Land of Patagonia

When the Spanish explorer Ferdinand Magellan discovered Patagonia in 1520, he started a rumor that persisted for several hundred years. He believed the island was inhabited by giants! Yes, the natives were a little taller than most Europeans, but to call them giants would be exaggerating a bit. Just imagine the tall tales those explorers told their friends and families about the Patagonian giants!

Patagonia is considered the jewel of Argentina, with a richly diverse landscape made up of mountains, rainforests, plains, lakes and rivers. Valued for its natural beauty, Patagonia is home to many unique animals that are not found anywhere else in the world.

Spheniscus Magellanicus

(Magellanic Penguin)

The Magellanic Penguins were discovered by Ferdinand Magellan in 1520 when he spotted millions of the black and white birds around the southern coast of Argentina. Though many of the penguins exist today, they are listed as a threatened species because of damage created by oil spills in the region.

Rhea pennata

(Patagonian Ostrich)

Named after the Greek goddess Rhea, the Patagonian Ostrich is a large flightless bird that can run at speeds up to 37 miles per hour! Now there's a bird you don't want to make enemies with!

Lama guanicoe

(Guanaco)

Living in the mountainous regions of Patagonia, these relatives of the camel can live to be 25 years old. The guanaco are excellent swimmers, and they have adapted to successfully living in rugged terrain where food is sometimes sparse. Their only natural predator is the mountain lion.

"Healthy citizens are the greatest asset any country can have."

"Healthy citizens are the greatest asset any country can have."

British Prime Minister, Winston Churchill

EUROPE
N
E
S
W
SCOTLAND - ITALY - GREECE - NETHERLANDS - POLAND

Scotland

The National Symbol of Scotland

The unicorn, believe it or not, is the national animal of Scotland. It has long stood as a symbol of the region, appearing on the royal coat of arms as early as the 1600s. But, you may still be wondering why an imaginary animal is the symbol for such a great nation.

Unicorns are fascinating characters in literary history and oral traditions in Europe. Although they are remarkably beautiful and elegant, they are also depicted as being extremely fierce, proud and unpredictable creatures. Stories often involve unicorns fighting to the death rather than experiencing slavery in captivity.

The Scottish people have come to feel a sort of kinship with the mythical creature as they've struggled to retain their freedom over the years. Represented in great works of art, tapestries hanging in royal palaces and even gold coins and currencies, the unicorn has found a special place in the hearts of the people of Scotland.

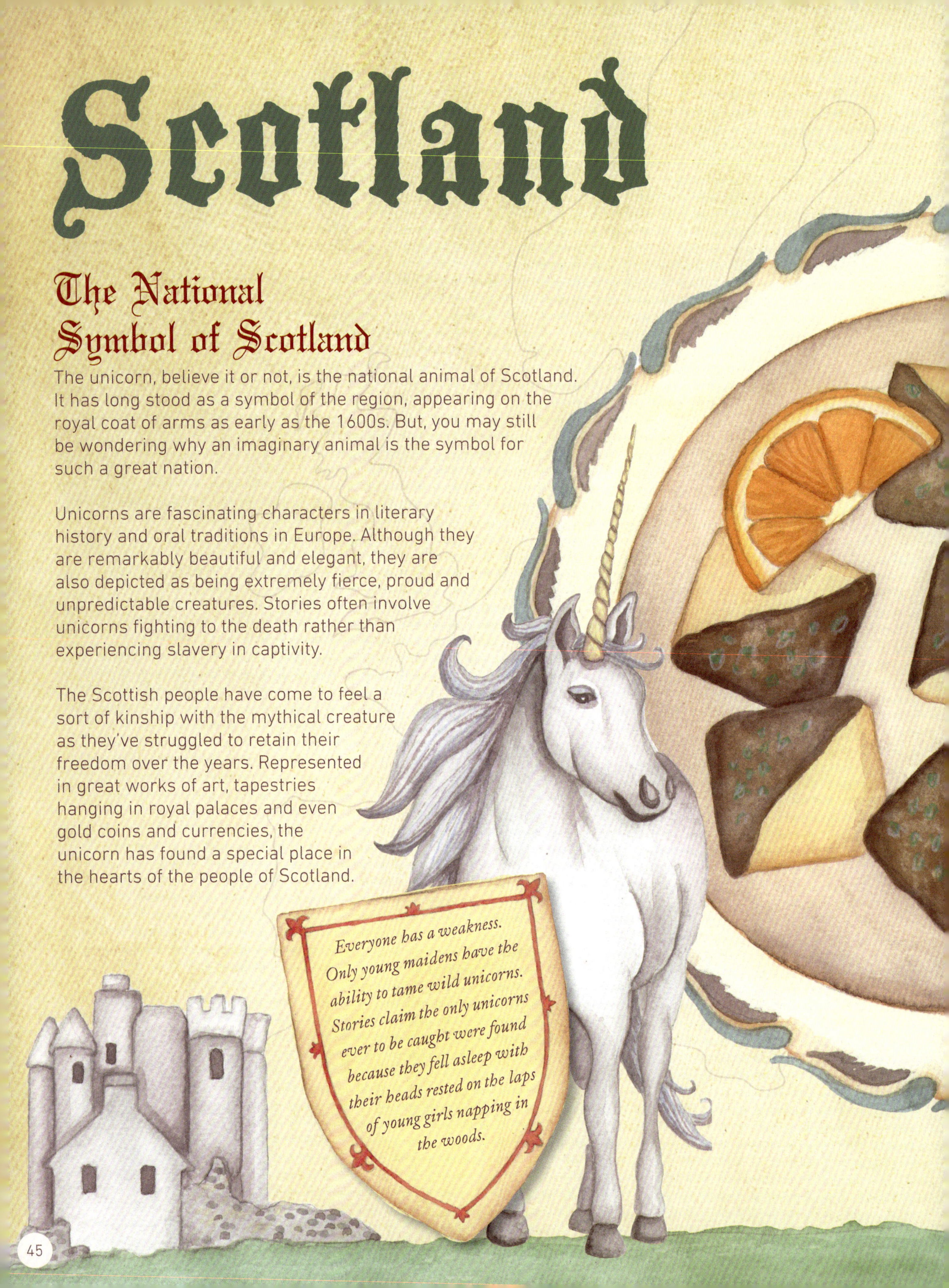

Everyone has a weakness. Only young maidens have the ability to tame wild unicorns. Stories claim the only unicorns ever to be caught were found because they fell asleep with their heads rested on the laps of young girls napping in the woods.

The Scottish Thistle

According to an ancient legend, Norse armies were invading Scotland many years ago. In the middle of the night when the Scottish army was fast asleep, a barefoot Norseman approaching their camp stepped on a thistle and cried out in pain. This alerted the Scottish army who woke from their sleep to defeat the invading army. Since then, the thistle has been become a symbol of nobility and Scottish heritage.

Shortbread Cookies

With only four ingredients, shortbread is quite possibly one of the simplest recipes you can make in the kitchen. However, it has anything but a simple history. The national dish has been prepared for royalty and nobility since the 12th century. Prestigious monarchs such as Mary, Queen of Scots and Queen Victoria referred to it as their favorite dessert — a required dish in their households for both Christmas and Scottish New Year.

In the 12th century, shortbread was a little different. Historically, the word "biscuit" meant twice-baked bread. Bakers would collect all the extra pieces of dough after making bread, and send it to the oven a second time to form hard, dry rounds of bread. Over time, butter was added to the recipe making it more of a commodity for people who could afford the nicer things in life. The large amount of butter in shortbread makes it the crispy and crumbly dessert we know today.

Adopted in the 12th century by William I, who was known as "William the Lion," the Red Lion has since become a national symbol of Scotland.

Shortbread Cookies

STEP BY STEP

1. Preheat the oven to 325 degrees Fahrenheit.

2. Sift the flour through a sieve into a small bowl. Set aside.

3. In a large bowl, cream together the butter, sugar and orange extract. Add the flour. Mix well. You may have to use your hands toward the end to get the mixture to form a ball.

4. Flatten the ball onto waxed or parchment paper and roll into a ½-inch thick rectangle. Use a small cookie cutter to cut out 2-inch squares. Place ½-inch apart on a parchment lined cookie sheet.

5. Bake for 14-16 minutes or until bottoms are light golden brown. Do not over bake.

6. In small bowl, microwave chocolate chips and shortening on High 1 to 1 1/2 minutes or until melted; stir until smooth. Once the shortbread has cooled, dip a portion of each cookie into the melted chocolate. Place on waxed paper until chocolate is set.

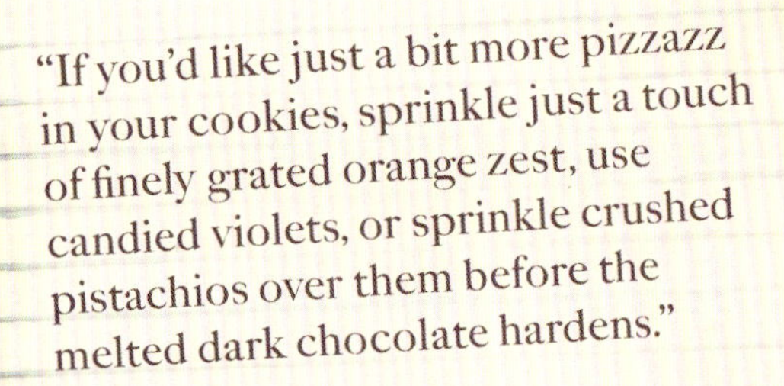

FROM THE AUTHOR

"If you'd like just a bit more pizzazz in your cookies, sprinkle just a touch of finely grated orange zest, use candied violets, or sprinkle crushed pistachios over them before the melted dark chocolate hardens."

WHAT YOU'LL NEED

INGREDIENTS

- 1 cup unsalted butter
- 3/4 cup powdered sugar
- 1 tablespoon orange extract
- 2 1/2 cups all-purpose flour
- 1 cup semisweet chocolate chips
- 2 tablespoons shortening

Nutrition Facts : Serving Size: (75g) | Servings: 12

	% Daily Value
Calories: 370 — Calories From Fat 200	
Total Fat: 22g	34%
Saturated Fat: 13g	65%
Trans Fat: 0g	
Cholesterol: 40mg	13%
Sodium: 0mg	0%
Total Carbohydrate: 41g	14%
Dietary Fiber: 2g	8%
Sugars: 18g	
Protein: 4g	

SCOTLAND

Capital City / Edinburgh

Nation Language / English

Population / 5,313,600

Currency / Pound sterling

Scotland is located in Europe and comprises the upper third of Great Britain. Forming a great peninsula, Scotland is surrounded by water on three sides: the Atlantic Ocean, the North Sea and the Irish Sea.

The Loch Ness Monster

A cryptid is the name of an animal whose existence has not been authenticated by the scientific community. We've heard of many cryptids in our time, including Bigfoot, the Abominable Snowman and of course the Loch Ness Monster.

There are few people in the world who haven't heard about the Loch Ness Monster of Scotland. The Loch Ness monster, or Nessie for short, is reported to be living in the profoundly deep body of water called Loch Ness. This vast body of water was created many years ago when a massive tremor caused the earth to open up along the Great Glen fault line. The Loch is reported to be 754 feet deep and two and a half miles long, with a bottom as flat as the playing field of a football stadium. All of this creates an environment perfectly suited for a giant sea monster!

Nessie has been sighted many times in the last 100 years by fisherman, residents and even tourists. However, no one has been able to provide conclusive evidence in the form of video footage, photos or tissue samples that would convince scientists the animal really exists. However, ask anyone living in the area surrounding the Loch; everyone has a story or knows someone who has a story about Nessie. She makes for an interesting legend, indeed.

What to look for:

Nessie has been described as anywhere from 18-50 feet long and greyish-black to dark brown in color. She has a barrel-shaped body and looks like the prehistoric plesiosaur. (An aquatic reptile that went extinct 65 million years ago)

Lochness monster - Nessiteras rhombopteryx

MASKS OF THE WORLD

Masks have been a part of important rituals and ceremonies in every corner of the globe since prehistoric times. Created from nearly every material known to man, ceremonial masks come in every shape, color and size. Depending on the culture, some masks are even thought to possess a power or magic of their own. Can you think of any occasions when we might wear masks in our culture?

AFRICA

Many African tribes feel it is easier for animals to communicate with spirits than man. Thus, animals are often incorporated into ceremonial mask designs. This West-African mask is carved out of teak, a hardwood regularly used for making masks.

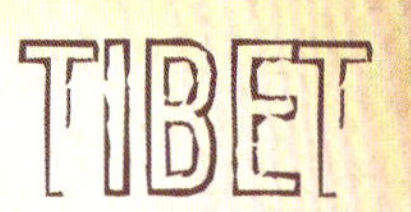

TIBET

This ceremonial mask was used in the 17th century in northern Tibet. The mask depicts Garuda, a powerful bird found in Buddhist mythology. Garuda is a powerful antidote against the negative influence of nagas "spirits," which the Tibetans believed might be responsible for illness and bad luck.

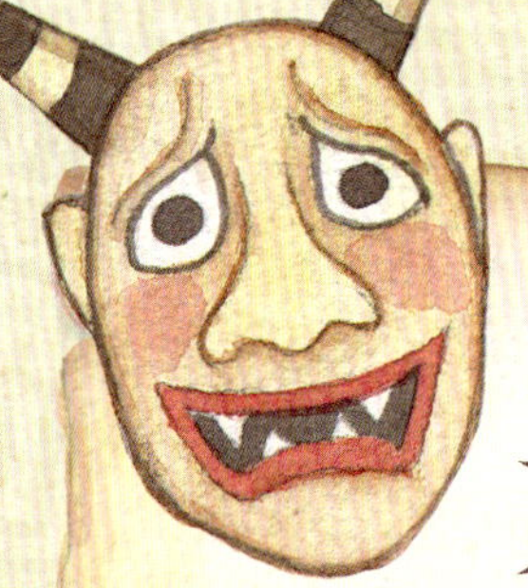

Peru

Celebrated in Bolivia and Peru, Danza de los Diablos "Dance of the Devils" features performers dressed in devil masks and costumes. Stylistically, the masks range from simple to incredibly ornate designs.

Green Man

Stemming from European folklore and pagan beliefs, the Green Man is a god who represents the spirits of the trees, plants and foliage. Depictions of the Green Man have been found in medieval art throughout Europe as well as great literary works such as Sir Gawain and the Green Knight.

Yup'ik Eskimo

The central Alaskan Yup'ik people are a nomadic Eskimo tribe living in western and southwestern Alaska. More than 22,000 members of the tribe exist today, and they continue to practice their traditional mask making. Once a mask is used for a ceremonial dance, it is destroyed and never used again.

Sri Lanka

Created by the native Sinhalese people of Sri Lanka, a mask of this nature is created to provide peace, harmony and wealth. Legend has it the country was once ruled by a mythical people called Raksasas. Although the Raksha people are long gone and may have never existed at all, their masks are still worn during traditional Sri Lankan dances. The fanciful blue creature in this mask is named Mayura, a peacock who provides transport for the Buddhist god Ceylon.

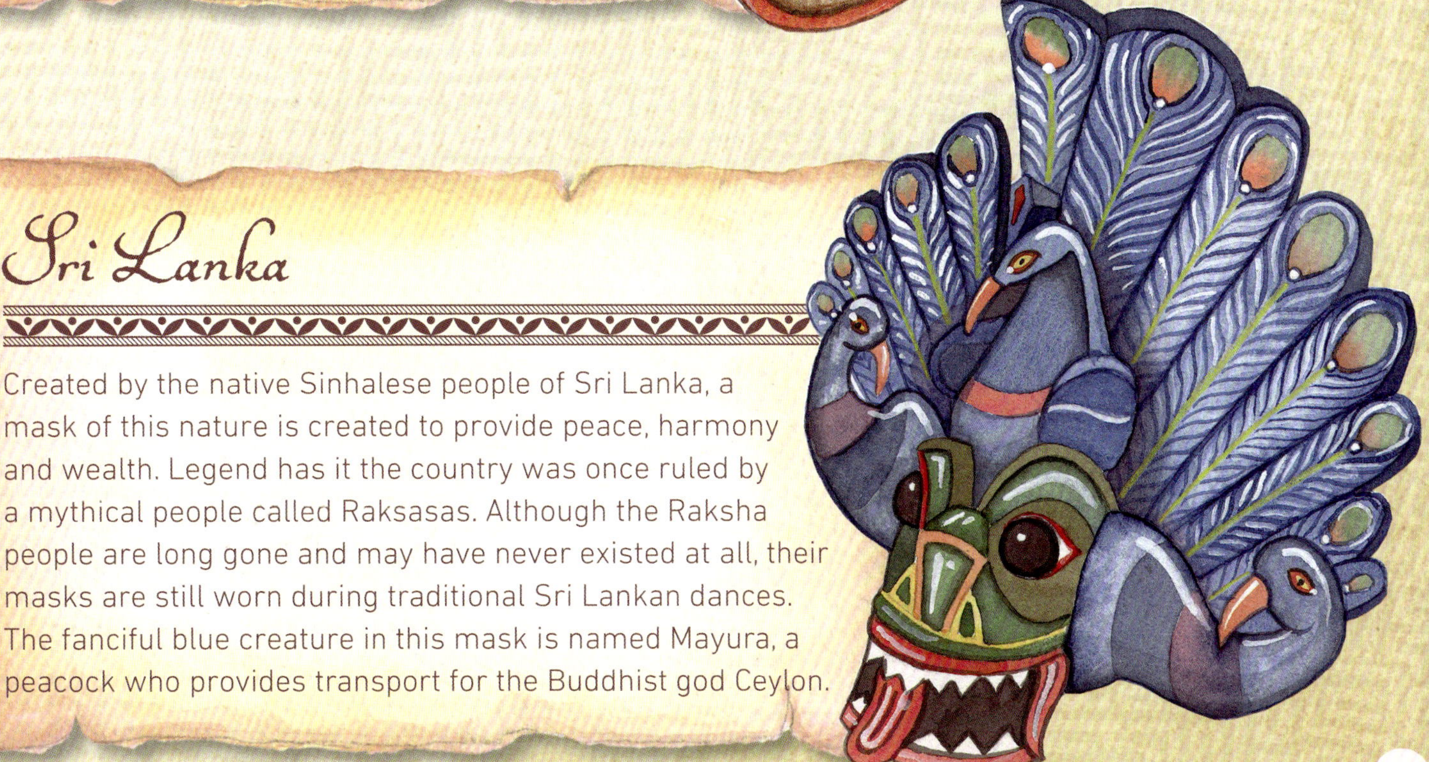

Italy

Medico della Peste

Based on a traditional Venetian Carnival design, the Medico della Peste (Plague Doctor Mask) wasn't originally intended for parties. It had a far more practical application and was used by doctors during the plague to prevent the spread of disease.

Carnival of Venice

Carnival in Venice is one of the crown jewels of Italian culture. Stepping off a gondola onto the city's cobblestone streets during Carnival is like walking into a fairy tale. The great city comes alive, bursting forth in bright colors, sequins and feathers, all belonging to a unique cast of costumed characters roaming the streets. The Venetian Carnival is one of the most unique celebrations in the world.

Almost every culture celebrates some version of Carnival, but in Italy the tradition is uniquely tied to the Catholic season of Lent. The faithful churchgoers are required to fast (to not eat certain foods) for six weeks prior to Easter every year. Thus, Carnival represents the final opportunity to indulge in the luxuries of expensive food and wine before the fast begins.

Referred to as il Tricolore, the colors of the Italian flag are said to represent hope (green), faith (white) and charity (red).

Caprese Salad
(Insalata Caprese)

Nothing is more enjoyable on a hot summer afternoon than a plate of Caprese Salad with tasty red tomatoes, fresh mozzarella and basil just picked from the garden! Chances are you've had this delicious treat before, but do you know its history?

There is a lot of mystery surrounding the creator of Italy's favorite salad, but we know one thing for sure; it was first seen on the menu at Quisisana Hotel on the Island of Capri in 1920, just after World War One. Most likely, a very patriotic cook whipped up this salad for the first time in honor of his country. The Caprese Salad is comprised of the colors of the Italian national flag, green, white and red.

Caprese Salad (Insalata Caprese)

Step by Step

1. Wash the tomatoes and basil. Assemble a cherry tomato, mozzarella ball and basil leaf for every skewer you want to make.

2. Insert the skewer through the tomato, basil and mozzarella, positioning the items securely, and leaving room to pick up the skewer later.

3. Assemble the Caprese skewers on a plate and drizzle lightly with olive oil.

4. Season with salt and pepper to taste.

5. To make a balsamic glaze, in a small pan, heat one cup of balsamic vinegar over medium-low heat. Stirring occasionally, allow the vinegar to come to a very gentle simmer. Cook for 10 minutes until the mixture becomes syrupy in consistency. Be careful not to burn the vinegar. Allow the glaze to cool, then drizzle on top of your skewers.

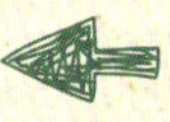

Sophie's Tip for Kids

"If you'd like to make a more portable version of Caprese, you can assemble and shake up all the ingredients in a medium size container with a lid. It makes an easy snack to take to a picnic, dinner at a friend's house or any special event."

What You'll Need

Ingredients

- 8 ounces cherry tomatoes
- 8 ounces fresh mozzarella balls
- 1 bunch fresh basil leaves
- Olive oil
- 1 cup balsamic vinegar (optional)
- Salt and pepper to taste
- Large toothpicks or small skewers

Nutrition Facts : Serving Size: (94g) | Servings: 6

	% Daily Value
Calories: 190	Calories From Fat 160
Total Fat: 18g	28%
Saturated Fat: 7g	35%
Trans Fat: 0g	
Cholesterol: 30mg	10%
Sodium: 25mg	1%
Total Carbohydrate: 2g	1%
Dietary Fiber: 1g	4%
Sugars: 1g	
Protein: 7g	

ITALY

Capital City / Rome

Nation Language / Italian

Population / 61,482,297

Currency / Euro

Italy is a long and narrow peninsula in southern Europe surrounded by the Mediterranean Sea. The country is famously shaped like a high-heeled boot kicking a ball, which is the Italian island of Sicily.

The Gondoliers of Venice

Did you know the entire city of Venice was built on a series of small islands and marshlands off the coast of Italy? The muddy coastal waters provided a safe haven from invaders hoping to steal the riches of the wealthy merchants that lived there. But the question was, how do you build a great city on the water? The Venetian founders needed to think a little differently. They drove great wooden spikes down into the thick mud to create foundations for their homes. And instead of regular paved streets, they created a series of waterways called canals.

Rarely is there a postcard of Italy that doesn't include scenes from beautiful Venice. A city unlike any other in the world, Venice is magical. Visitors from all over the world descend upon Italy to experience the wonder of Venice for themselves. The canals are full of boats traveling in every direction, carrying tourists and locals alike.

Just like a big city needs taxis and taxi drivers, Venice needs gondolas and gondoliers. A gondola is like a water taxi, and a gondolier is a specially trained person who propels and steers the gondola along the narrow and busy canals throughout the city. The city of Venice limits the number of gondolier licenses to 450, which makes for fierce competition when a gondolier dies. To make things more interesting, a gondolier can pass his license on to his son when he retires or dies.

Hippocrates

GREECE

Ancient Greece

Many of the crowning achievements of Western civilization can be traced back to the ancient Greeks who prospered during the Classical period of 500-336 BC. Many important ideas about medicine, government, theatre, art and architecture were birthed during this time. The list of achievements during the period is endless, with many modern conveniences such as the alarm clock, the shower, vending machines and umbrellas invented due to Greek discoveries.

Aesop's Fables

The collection of tales we know as Aesop's Fables have been enjoyed by children and adults alike for more than 2,000 years. Perhaps you've heard some of the stories? The Boy Who Cried Wolf, The Tortoise and the Hare, The Goose that Laid the Golden Egg, and the Lion and the Mouse are all stories told by a man named Aesop (620-560 BC).

There is a lot of debate over details about Aesop's life. He has been depicted as both a dwarf with a crooked nose and bent back as well as a black man from Ethiopia. What we know for sure is that Aesop's fables have influenced millions of readers and provided inspiration for many popular children's books today.

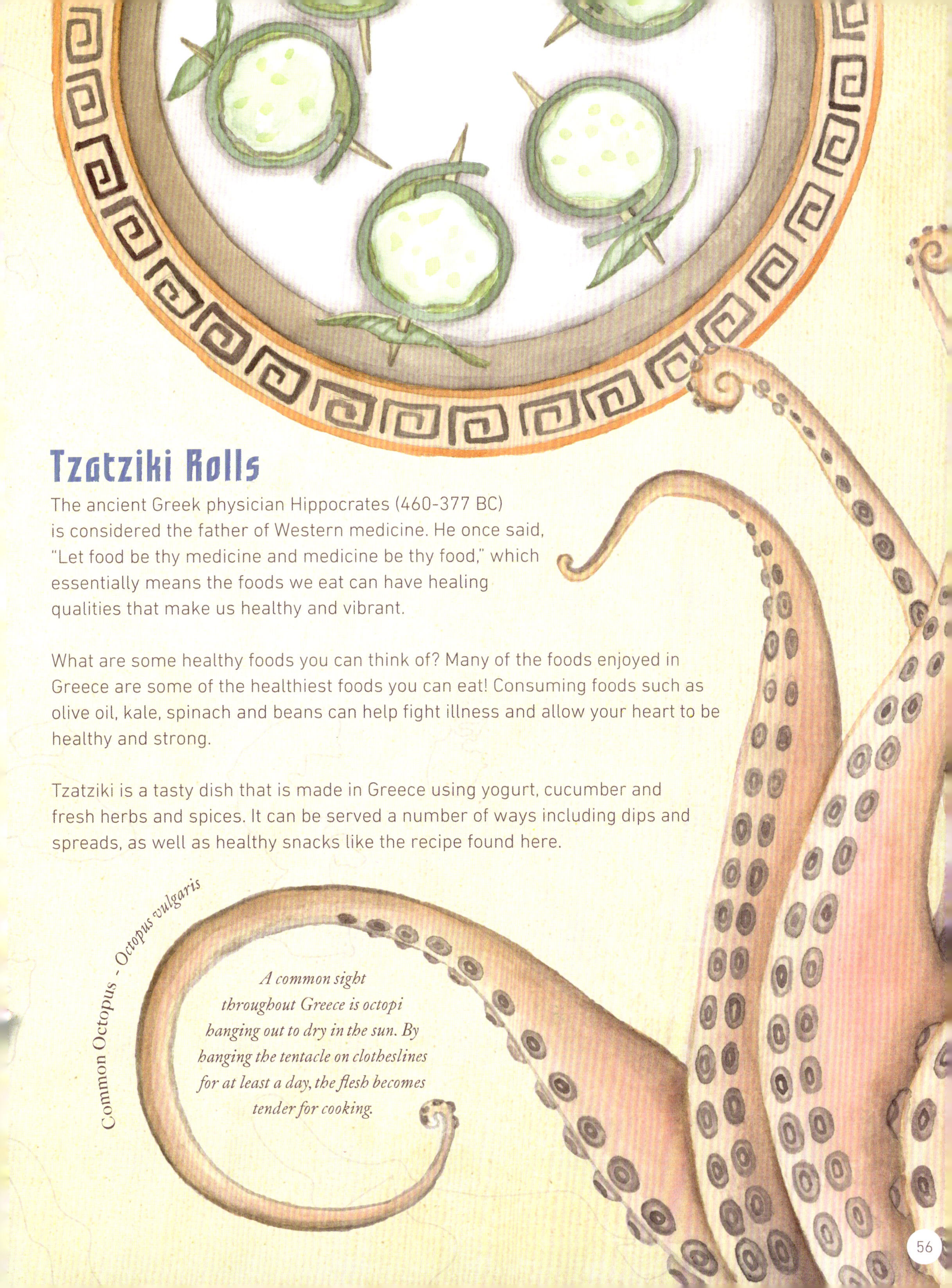

Tzatziki Rolls

The ancient Greek physician Hippocrates (460-377 BC) is considered the father of Western medicine. He once said, "Let food be thy medicine and medicine be thy food," which essentially means the foods we eat can have healing qualities that make us healthy and vibrant.

What are some healthy foods you can think of? Many of the foods enjoyed in Greece are some of the healthiest foods you can eat! Consuming foods such as olive oil, kale, spinach and beans can help fight illness and allow your heart to be healthy and strong.

Tzatziki is a tasty dish that is made in Greece using yogurt, cucumber and fresh herbs and spices. It can be served a number of ways including dips and spreads, as well as healthy snacks like the recipe found here.

Common Octopus - *Octopus vulgaris*

A common sight throughout Greece is octopi hanging out to dry in the sun. By hanging the tentacle on clotheslines for at least a day, the flesh becomes tender for cooking.

Tzatziki Rolls

STEP BY STEP

1. Cut the ends off the English cucumbers and slice lengthwise at about 1/8 inch thickness. Note: You'll want the strips of cucumber to be thin enough they can be flexible, but thick enough that they won't fall apart.

2. Lightly sprinkle salt over each side of the cucumber strips and leave them for 10 minutes.

3. In a small mixing bowl, stir in the yogurt, lemon juice, garlic cloves, dill and mint until evenly mixed.

4. Rinse the cucumber strips and pat them dry using a paper towel.

5. Lay the cucumber strip flat, spoon a small scoop of yogurt mixture at the end of the cucumber strip and roll using a toothpick to hold the strip and mint garnish in place. Repeat until mixture runs out.

SOPHIE'S TIP FOR KIDS

"If you don't want to make rolls, try making little cucumber sandwiches by slicing the cucumbers into coins instead. Place a layer of yogurt mix between two cucumber coins to form a little sandwich! Or use the coins like chips to dip into the yogurt mixture."

WHAT YOU'LL NEED

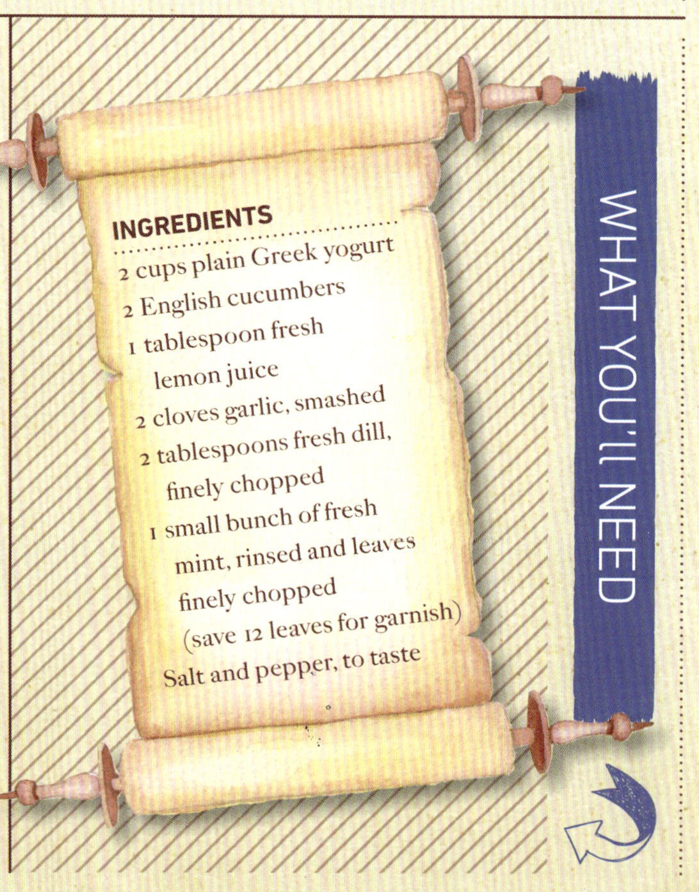

INGREDIENTS
2 cups plain Greek yogurt
2 English cucumbers
1 tablespoon fresh lemon juice
2 cloves garlic, smashed
2 tablespoons fresh dill, finely chopped
1 small bunch of fresh mint, rinsed and leaves finely chopped (save 12 leaves for garnish)
Salt and pepper, to taste

Nutrition Facts : Serving Size: (90g) | Servings: 12

	% Daily Value
Calories: 60 — Calories From Fat 35	
Total Fat: 4g	6%
Saturated Fat: 3g	15%
Trans Fat: 0g	
Cholesterol: 5mg	2%
Sodium: 10mg	0%
Total Carbohydrate: 3g	1%
Dietary Fiber: 1g	4%
Sugars: 2g	
Protein: 3g	

GREECE

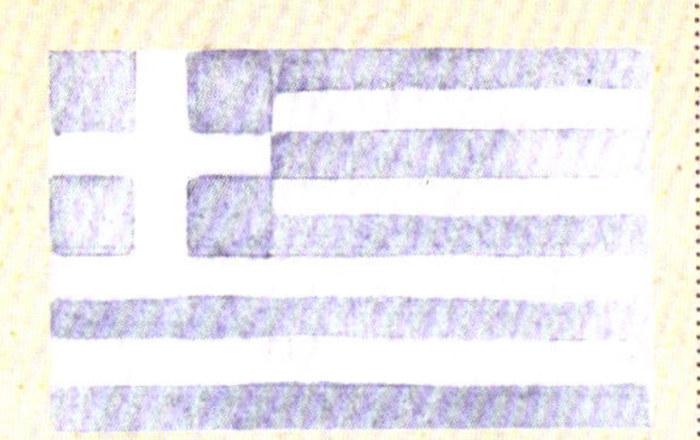

Capital City / Athens

Nation Language / Greek

Population / 10,772,967

Currency / Euro

Greece is comprised of a mainland peninsula and an astounding 1,400 islands scattered throughout the Mediterranean Sea. Only 169 of the islands actually have people living on them, the largest two being Crete and Euboea.

Zeus, the King of Greek Mythology

Have you ever wondered why good and bad things happen and why you don't seem to have much control over those events? The ancient Greeks had those thoughts as well, and they answered their questions by telling stories about an enchanted family of gods who ruled heaven and earth.

Zeus was the king of all the gods and the father of all men. More powerful than any other gods, he could throw his voice, shape shift and toss lightning bolts through the sky at wrongdoers. He is represented as the god of mercy and justice, the protector of the meek and the punisher of the unjust.

The stories the ancient Greeks told have become known as mythology. Their stories explained the nature of people and science and helped them understand life in general. Because they believed the gods could directly affect the lives of humans, it was important to know the personalities and characteristics of each of the gods so they wouldn't unknowingly offend them.

HOUSES OF THE WORLD

Not everyone lives in a wooden house with three bedrooms, two bathrooms and a kitchen. In fact, the traditional American home is far from the norm in places like Guatemala where a home is usually one or two rooms with a dirt floor. When reviewing the homes in this section, consider why each home is built the way it is. What is the weather like in the region? What is the economic situation? Learning about homes around the world provides a wonderful glimpse into life in other countries.

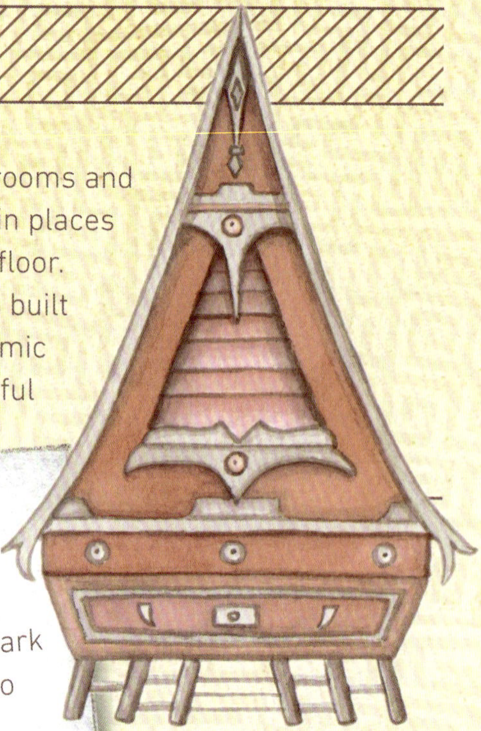

Jabu: In North Sumatra, Indonesia, the Batak Toba people live in wooden boat-like structures on stilts called jabu. With a high thatched roof and only one small window on each side, the home stays pretty dark inside, making it a great place to sleep. Families who live in a jabu spend most of their time outside.

Beehive Houses: the heat in the Middle East can be incredibly difficult to bear, therefore Syrian beehive houses use natural elements such as mud, dirt, straw and stones to better protect themselves from the heat. Syrian homes in this style have been continuously built since 3700 BC.

Yurt: Yurts are circular tent-like structures with bent rods supporting the roof, and lattice providing support for the walls. The entire structure is covered with fabric and sheep's wool to make the interior weatherproof and warm. The portable nature of yurts has benefitted nomadic tribes in Central Asia for several thousand years.

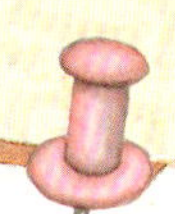

Turf Houses: Turf homes in Iceland have been built for over 1,000 years as a way of dealing with the difficult and cold climate. First a flat stone foundation is laid out, then a traditional wooden structure with a steep-pitched roof is built. Finally, the house is surrounded and topped with turf (grass with dirt and roots attached) that acts as insulation.

Igloo: The igloo is a home built out of blocks of ice and snow and is primarily used by the Inuit people (commonly known as Eskimo) in Canada and parts of Alaska. Even in temperatures well below zero, the igloo can maintain a temperature of 19 to 60 degrees Fahrenheit based solely on the body heat created by the people sleeping inside.

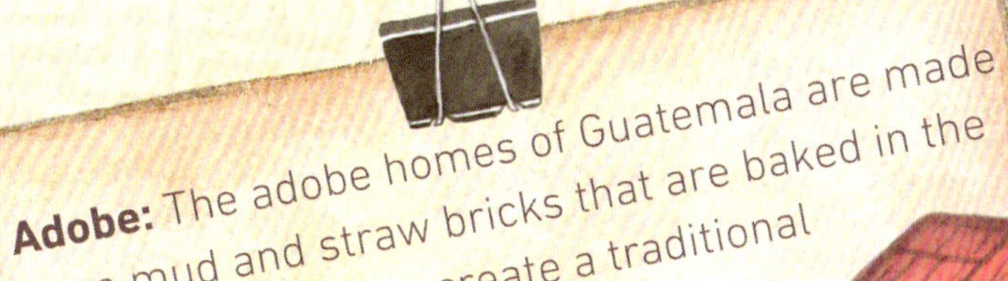

Adobe: The adobe homes of Guatemala are made from mud and straw bricks that are baked in the sun then stacked to create a traditional house with four walls. The structures usually have a tile or tin roof. Homes like these can be found in all parts of Mexico and Central America and are usually painted in an assortment of bright colors.

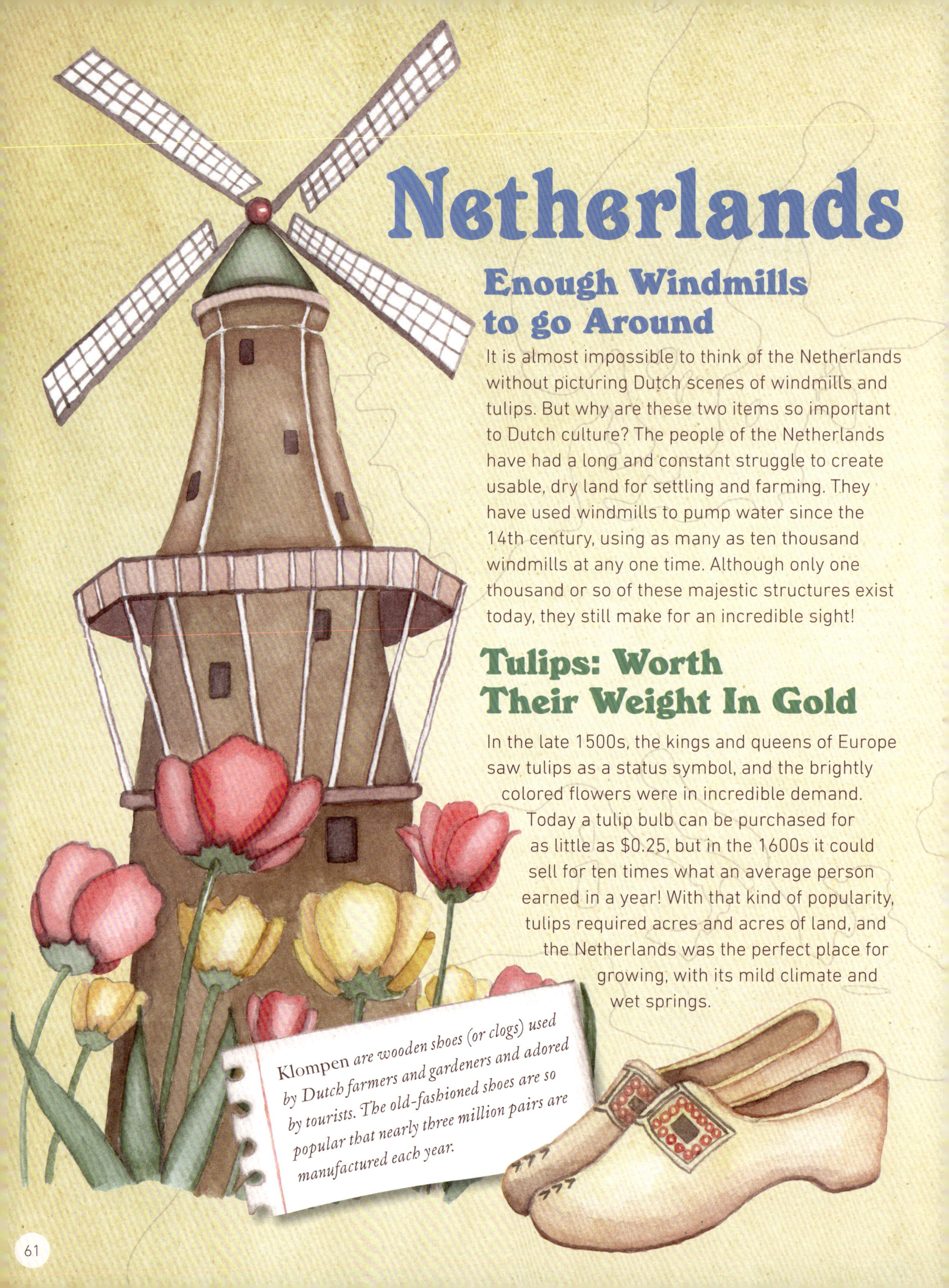

Netherlands

Enough Windmills to go Around

It is almost impossible to think of the Netherlands without picturing Dutch scenes of windmills and tulips. But why are these two items so important to Dutch culture? The people of the Netherlands have had a long and constant struggle to create usable, dry land for settling and farming. They have used windmills to pump water since the 14th century, using as many as ten thousand windmills at any one time. Although only one thousand or so of these majestic structures exist today, they still make for an incredible sight!

Tulips: Worth Their Weight In Gold

In the late 1500s, the kings and queens of Europe saw tulips as a status symbol, and the brightly colored flowers were in incredible demand. Today a tulip bulb can be purchased for as little as $0.25, but in the 1600s it could sell for ten times what an average person earned in a year! With that kind of popularity, tulips required acres and acres of land, and the Netherlands was the perfect place for growing, with its mild climate and wet springs.

Klompen *are wooden shoes (or clogs) used by Dutch farmers and gardeners and adored by tourists. The old-fashioned shoes are so popular that nearly three million pairs are manufactured each year.*

Dutch Pea Soup "Snert" (Erwtensoep)

What comes to mind when you hear the word "Snert"? Would you ever guess that it's the name for a delicious bacon and pea soup from the Netherlands? The Dutch have been preparing Snert for a long time, often enjoying a bowl during the long, cold winter months.

Although the Dutch perfected it, pea soup has been around for a really long time. The Greek playwright Aristophanes referred to it in his play "The Birds" around the year 400 BC because it was commonly sold in the markets of Athens. In fact, this dish is so popular you can find references to it in almost every culture around the world. You may have heard the famous poem from England that reads, "Pease porridge hot, Pease porridge cold, Pease porridge in the pot, Nine days old."

Anne Frank: The Diary of a Young Girl

Anne Frank might be one of the most famous fifteen-year-olds the world has ever known. When she died in March 1945, one of the many Jewish victims of the Holocaust, she left behind a journal detailing her family's struggles to hide during the German occupation of the Netherlands. It has since become one of the most widely read journals in the world, giving readers worldwide a glimpse into war and its impact on human life. Anne's diary has been printed in 50 languages and has sold more than 25 million copies.

Go to AnneFrank.org to find out more about this amazing young woman.

Snert (Erwtensoep)

STEP BY STEP

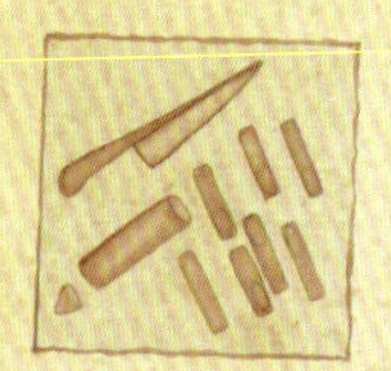

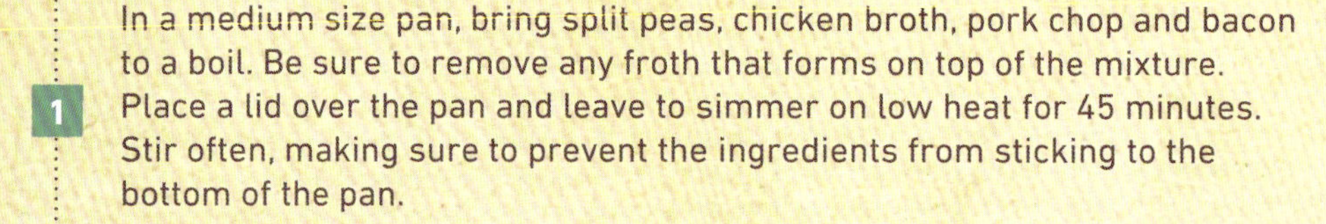

1 In a medium size pan, bring split peas, chicken broth, pork chop and bacon to a boil. Be sure to remove any froth that forms on top of the mixture. Place a lid over the pan and leave to simmer on low heat for 45 minutes. Stir often, making sure to prevent the ingredients from sticking to the bottom of the pan.

2 Take the pork chop and bacon out, debone and cut all the meat thinly. Set aside.

3 Add the onion, leek, carrot, celery, celery root and potato to the split pea mixture. Allow to boil for another 30 minutes.

4 When the vegetables become fork tender, puree half of the mixture in a blender. Return the blended material as well as the pork chop and bacon to the pot and mix well. If you like your soup chunky, puree only a quarter of the soup mixture.

5 Dice the kielbasa and mix with the soup several minutes before serving.

SOPHIE'S TIP FOR KIDS

"Don't make such a nasty face! Eating Snert can be a lot of fun, especially if you design a smiley face on the surface of the soup with just a little bit of sour cream."

Nutrition Facts : Serving Size: (407g) | Servings: 6

		% Daily Value
Calories: 440	Calories From Fat 110	
Total Fat: 12g		18%
Saturated Fat: 3.5g		18%
Trans Fat: 0g		
Cholesterol: 35mg		12%
Sodium: 440mg		18%
Total Carbohydrate: 56g		19%
Dietary Fiber: 16g		64%
Sugars: 10g		
Protein: 28g		

INGREDIENTS

- 11 ounces dried split peas
- 4 cups chicken stock
- 1 pork chop, 6 ounces
- 4 ounces bacon (or 6 slices)
- 1 small onion, finely diced
- 4 ounces leeks, finely diced
- 4 ounces carrots, diced
- 4 ounces celery root (leave it out if you can't find it)
- 1 large potato, peeled and diced
- 2 stalks celery, chopped
- Optional: 1, 14-ounce kielbasa, diced

NETHERLANDS

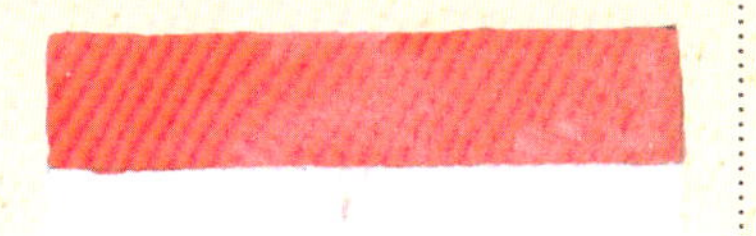

Capital City / Amsterdam

Nation Language / Dutch

Population / 16,788,973

Currency / Euro

The Netherlands is situated in a flat region of Europe where most of the land lies below sea level. It is reported that more than 65 percent of the country would be under water if it weren't for nearly 1,500 miles of dykes that prevent the North Sea from flooding the country.

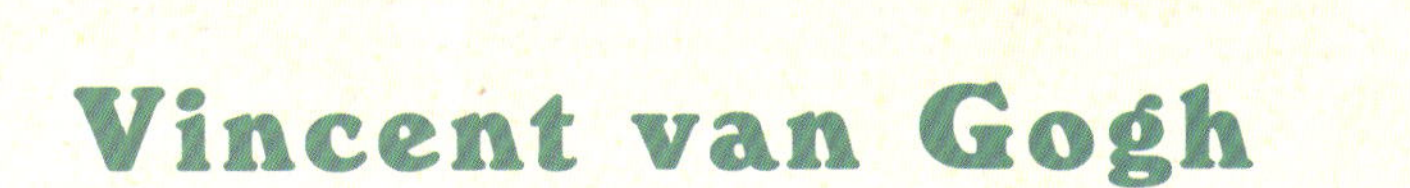

Vincent van Gogh

The Netherlands has had its fair share of famous artists. The 17th century was known as "The Age of the Dutch Masters" when the region claimed many important painters including Rembrandt and Vermeer.

Vincent van Gogh is one of the most famous Dutch artists, known both for his post-impressionistic style and his wild bouts of anxiety and depression. Deeply troubled his entire life, van Gogh channeled his passion and anxiety through his work. Take a moment to do a web search on Vincent van Gogh and get to know his paintings. It's likely that you've already seen a van Gogh painting without realizing it was his.

Among van Gogh's most famous paintings is The Starry Night. The night landscape in this painting comes to life with stars and light swirling and dancing off the page. How does it make you feel to know the artist painted this masterpiece while he was under considerable stress? Though van Gogh only lived to be 37, he left behind a wealth of material with more than 2,100 works of art.

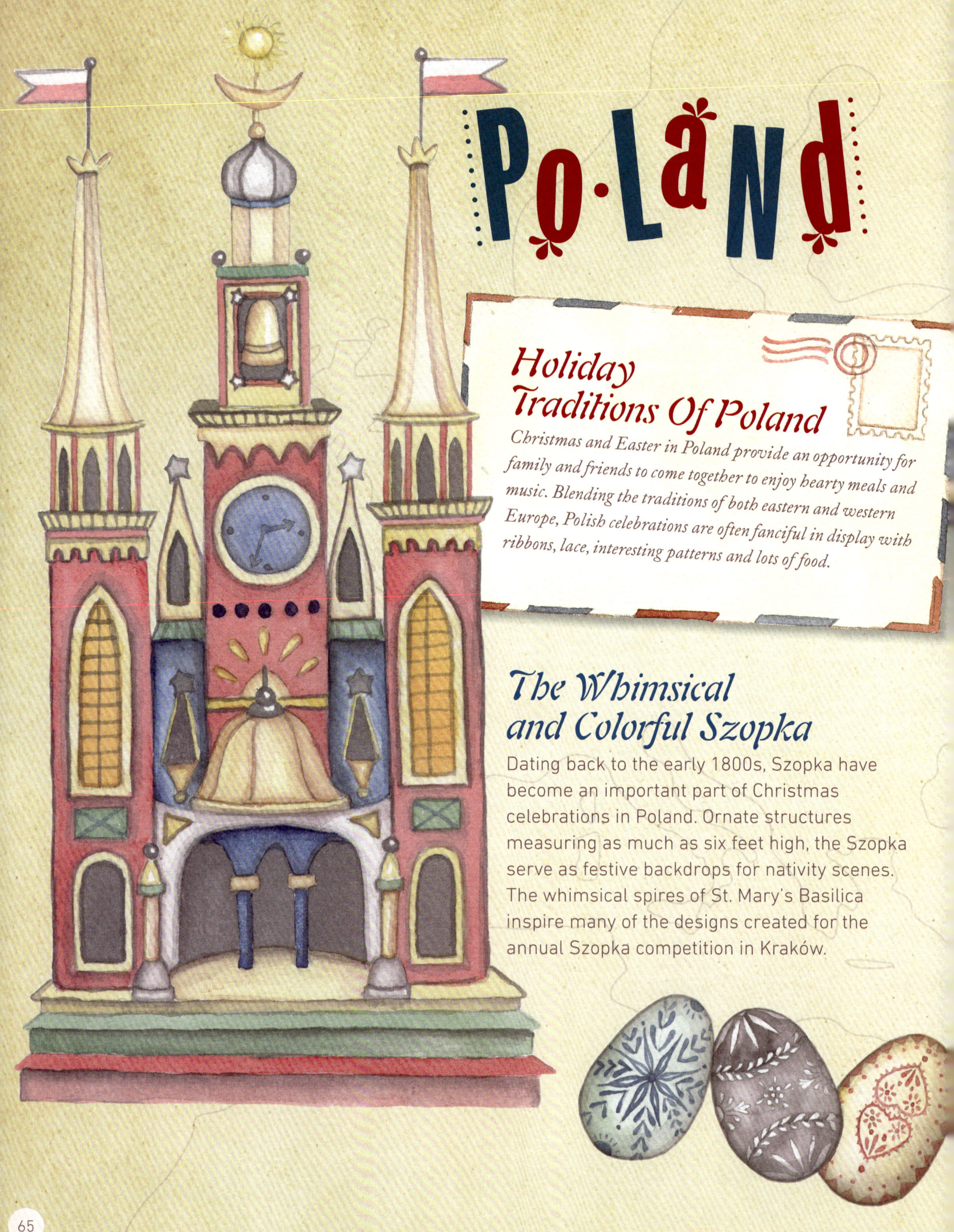

PO·LAND

Holiday Traditions Of Poland

Christmas and Easter in Poland provide an opportunity for family and friends to come together to enjoy hearty meals and music. Blending the traditions of both eastern and western Europe, Polish celebrations are often fanciful in display with ribbons, lace, interesting patterns and lots of food.

The Whimsical and Colorful Szopka

Dating back to the early 1800s, Szopka have become an important part of Christmas celebrations in Poland. Ornate structures measuring as much as six feet high, the Szopka serve as festive backdrops for nativity scenes. The whimsical spires of St. Mary's Basilica inspire many of the designs created for the annual Szopka competition in Kraków.

Polanaise *is the name of a special Polish dance performed as an opening event of a Studniówka (Polish high school prom). This event takes place one hundred days before final exams.*

Angel Wings

(Chrusciki)

These delicious dessert items have enjoyed widespread appeal throughout history. They are available in many countries worldwide, and each region offers its own traditions and local names. Light and crispy with a dusting of powdered sugar, Angel Wings are enjoyed in Polish households during Easter and other special occasions. They truly are the perfect treat for any special event.

A Good Egg

Pisanki (Painted Polish Eggs) have been an important part of the Polish Easter celebrations for over a thousand years. The beautiful designs are created by first dipping an egg into hot wax, which forms a seal around it. After the wax hardens, an ornate design is scratched into it and then the egg is dipped into dye. The dye only adheres to the egg where the wax has been removed, creating a beautiful pattern.

What's In a Name?

In the United States they're known as Angel Wings, but in Poland they're known as Chrusciki. Depending upon whom you ask, the word means broken, dry twigs or brushwood. That makes sense if you think about it. Imagine walking through the ancient Białowieża Forest in Poland, and hearing the sound of dry twigs crackling and breaking under your feet. That's exactly what eating an Angel Wing sounds like!

Angel Wings (Chrusciki)

STEP BY STEP

1 In a medium size mixing bowl, cut butter into the flour until the mixture resembles coarse crumbs.

2 In a separate bowl, beat egg yolks with the sour cream and vanilla. Add to flour mixture, mix, then refrigerate overnight.

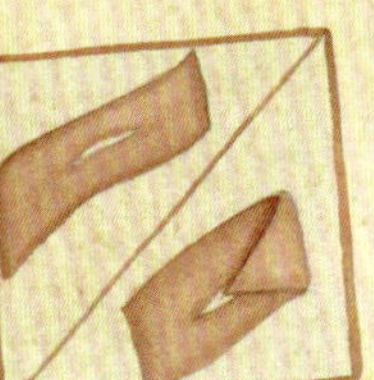

3 Preheat oven to 350 degrees Fahrenheit. Roll dough out to ¼ inch thickness on a flat surface. Cut into 1½-inch by 3-inch rectangles.

4 Make a 1-inch slit centered into each rectangle. Pull a corner through to make a bowtie or angel wing.

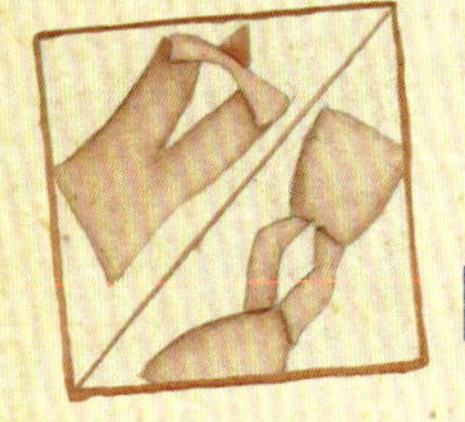

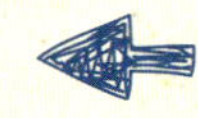

5 Place Angel Wings 1-inch apart on a parchment lined baking sheet, bake for 7-10 minutes or until golden brown. Sprinkle with powdered sugar when cool.

FROM THE AUTHOR

"Chrusciki are typically deep fried in oil or lard in order to get their trademark crispiness. If you're looking for an absolutely traditional experience, feel free to Google "Chrusciki Recipe" in order to find a recipe for the fried version."

WHAT YOU'LL NEED

INGREDIENTS

2 cups flour
1/2 cup sour cream
1/2 cup sugar
3 egg yolks
1/2 pound butter
1 teaspoon vanilla
Powdered sugar

Nutrition Facts : Serving Size: (45g) | Servings: 18

	% Daily Value
Calories: 200 — Calories From Fat 110	
Total Fat: 12g	18%
Saturated Fat: 3g	15%
Trans Fat: 2g	
Cholesterol: 35mg	12%
Sodium: 100mg	4%
Total Carbohydrate: 20g	7%
Dietary Fiber: 0g	7%
Sugars: 9g	
Protein: 2g	

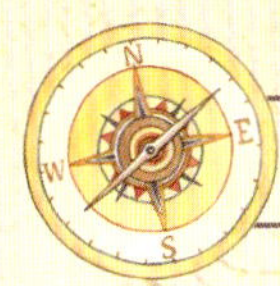

POLAND

Capital City / Warsaw

Nation Language / Polish

Population / 38,383,809

Currency / Złoty (PLN)

Poland derived its name from the Slavic tribe that once lived in the flatlands of western Poland. The tribe's name, Polonia, translates as "the people living in the fields."

The Legend of Baba Yaga

Baba Yaga is a complicated character; a twisted old witch who lives deep in the heart of the forest of Poland. Throughout history she's been depicted as living in a rambling old shack that hops around on chicken legs. Sometimes her house spins in circles to keep visitors from finding the front door, a spooky surprise for newcomers.

If Baba Yaga is having a bad day and doesn't want to talk to you, she'll fly away in her magical mortar and pestle, disappearing deep into the forest with no hopes of finding her again. In other words, you'll be pretty lucky if you get any face-to-face time with the fickle old lady.

Baba Yaga has answers for even the most difficult of questions. Rumor has it she ages one year for every question she is asked, so you can imagine any reluctance she may have to meeting you. The rare and magical blue rose helps Baba Yaga turn back the hands of time, so don't worry, she'll be around for many years to come.

Take a word of advice: if you see Baba Yaga deep in the forest, run in the opposite direction and you'll live to see another day!

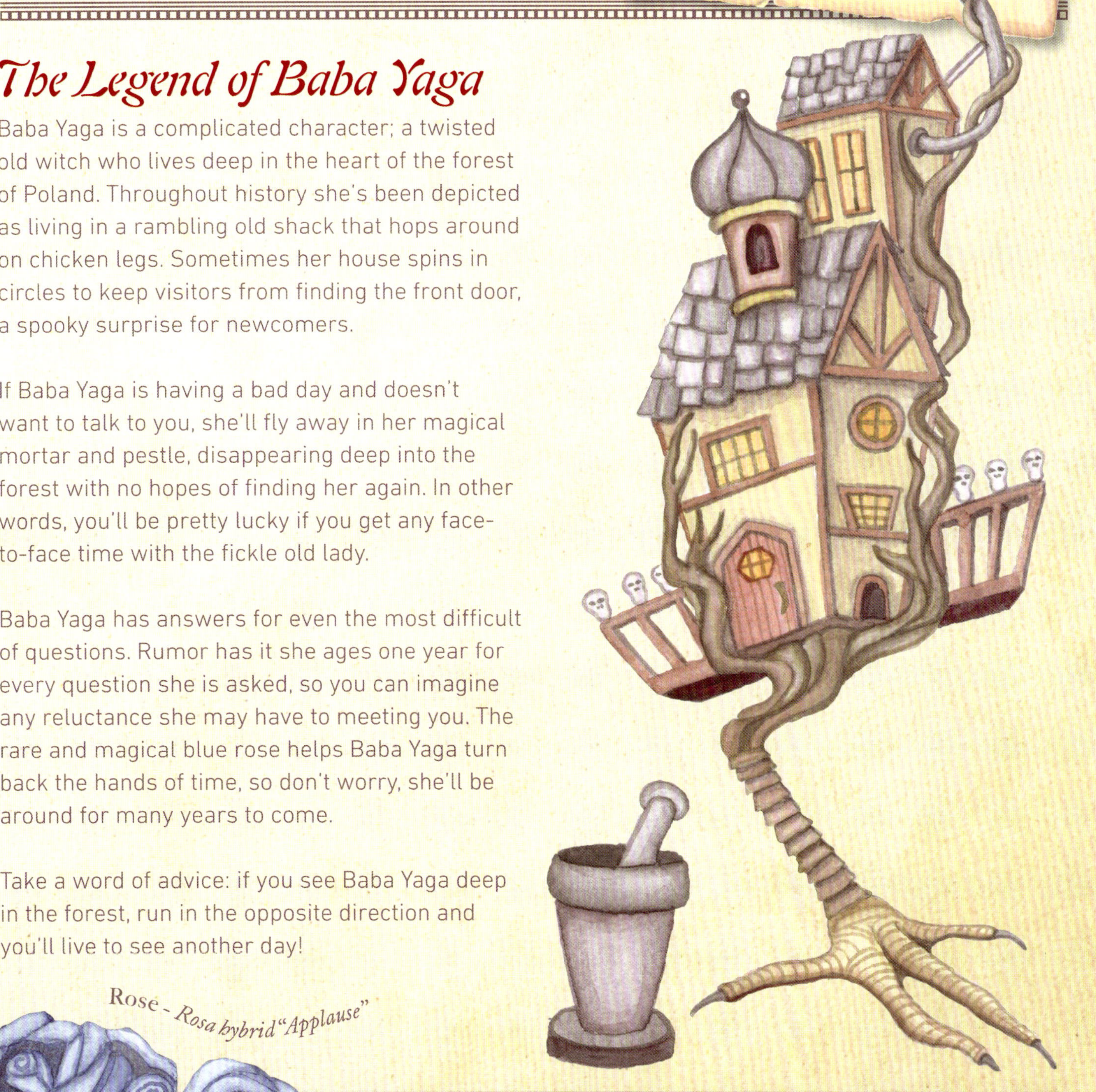

Rose - *Rosa hybrid "Applause"*

"An old pond -
a frog tumbles in -
the sound of water."

Japanese Poet, Matsuo Basho

ASIA
N
E
W
S
INDIA - THAILAND

INDIA

Om: *(the symbol of Hinduism) The sound "Om" represents energy in its simplest form, describing the essence of everything that is pure and natural.*

Hindu Gods and Goddesses of India

More than 80 percent of India practices a religion called Hinduism, which is the third largest religion in the world. Hinduism is unique in that it isn't based on the teachings of one specific teacher, and believers aren't required to follow a specific set of rules. Simply put, Hinduism is a way of living life.

Brahmā is the primary god in the Hindu religion, though he is experienced in the form of many gods and goddesses with varying responsibilities. Even though these other gods exist, they and Brahmā are considered one and the same.

Saraswati *is the goddess of knowledge, music and the arts.*

Diwali *is known as the Hindu Festival of Lights, an event where thousands of small, decorative lamps are lit representing the triumph of good over evil.*

Lakshmi *is the goddess of wealth and prosperity.*
Ganesha *is the god of intellect and the remover of obstacles.*
10 RS
INDIA POSTAGE

Mahatma Gandhi *said, "If we could change ourselves, the tendencies in the world would also change." He was one of the most important leaders in the fight for independence from England, well-known for his belief in non-violent activism.*

Cucumber and Lime Salad

(Khamang Kakdi)

Khamang Kakdi is a traditional recipe originating from the Maharashtra region in western India. Although ancient poems indicate the Maharashtra region was once only inhabited by exiled criminals and holy men, it is now the second largest state in India. What a difference 3,000 years can make!

The Maharashtrians (or Marathi people) practice the Hindu religion where a number of holy days require people not to eat any food (fasting). Fasting can be pretty tough for a lot of people, so there are a handful of food items the Marathi can eat, including this cucumber and lime salad.

Cucumber and Lime Salad (Khamang Kakdi)

1 In a large bowl, place cucumber, peanuts, two tablespoons of coconut, lime juice and agave syrup together.

2 In a small sauté pan, heat the oil. Add mustard seeds, stirring them until they start to crackle and pop. At this point add the cumin, salt and remaining coconut and continue stirring until the ingredients are evenly mixed. Turn off the heat.

3 Pour the sauté pan contents over the cucumber mixture, add cilantro and mix until the cucumbers are evenly coated. Season with salt or additional agave syrup until the mixture has your desired salty-sweet ratio.

SOPHIE'S TIP FOR KIDS

"Traditionally this recipe includes one finely chopped Serrano pepper, but that's too hot for me! If you like spicy food you can add chopped pepper to the sauté pan to spice things up."

Nutrition Facts : Serving Size: (128g) | Servings: 4

		% Daily Value
Calories: 300	Calories From Fat 240	
Total Fat: 27g		42%
Saturated Fat: 9g		45%
Trans Fat: 0g		
Cholesterol: 0mg		0%
Sodium: 590mg		25%
Total Carbohydrate: 10g		3%
Dietary Fiber: 5g		20%
Sugars: 4g		
Protein: 8g		

INGREDIENTS

- 1 English cucumber, cubed, 3-4 cups
- 2/3 cup shelled peanuts, finely chopped
- 1/2 cup unsweetened coconut, shredded
- 2 tablespoons fresh lime juice
- 1/2 teaspoon agave syrup
- 2 tablespoons olive oil
- 1/2 cup cilantro, finely chopped
- 1/2 teaspoon brown mustard seeds
- 1/2 teaspoon cumin
- 1/2 teaspoon salt
- 1/2 teaspoon cayenne pepper

INDIA

Capital City / New Delhi

Nation Language / Hindi /English

Population / 1,210,193,422

Currency / India Rupee

India is one of the most populated countries in the world, second only to China, with over 1.2 billion people calling it home. It is projected India's population will surpass China's before the year 2030, when it is expected to reach 1.6 billion people.

Mehndi: An Indian Wedding Tradition

Lawsonia inermis - Commonly known as Henna, this flowering plant is prized for the dye made from its crushed and powdered leaves. Used worldwide for cosmetic purposes such as dying hair and fabric, it is mostly used for making henna tattoos, known as Mehndi.

According to Hindu tradition, both men and women have been using henna to create ceremonial tattoos since ancient times in India. Typically the mehndi ceremony takes place several days before a marriage ceremony. The event is a festive celebration with women wearing bright, colorful dresses and performing traditional dances. There is lively music and lots of food for everyone.

The henna paste is applied to the hands and feet forming intricate patterns that include important Hindu symbolism as well as the names of the bride and groom. It can take many hours for a mehndi design to be applied, but when complete it can last for several weeks. In fact, tradition states the longer a mehndi design lasts, the longer the new wife can refrain from doing housework.

ACTIVITIES FOR THE KITCHEN

What Are Chopsticks Used For?

Research how people around the world eat their food. You can introduce new and fun ideas to your family and begin practicing dining customs from around the world. For example, when you cook and eat Asian food, use chopsticks. When eating foods from some African cultures, you are even supposed to eat with your hands! Visit your local library and talk with the librarians there about how to find books about different cultures.

How Much Does it Weigh?

Get your hands on a food scale whether you buy one or borrow one. Spend some time weighing different food items from your kitchen. Weigh several different kinds of foods in the same measuring cup and notice how much difference in weight there can be. For example, two cups of dry cereal will not weigh the same as two cups of flour.

How Much Will it Cost?

Go shopping—even if you have all the ingredients for your recipe. You do not have to buy anything. Just pay attention to how much the items cost and the total weight or amount. Then work out how much the amount of each ingredient will cost for your recipe. For example, say Greek yogurt is $5.27 for a quart-sized container and you want to figure out how much it will cost for the 2 cups you need to make Tzatziki Rolls on page 57-58 in the Greece section of this book.

First, check your measurement conversion chart. Two cups equals one pint. Two pints equals one quart. So, in this case you will need 1/2 of the total amount in the container for your recipe. Second, do the math:

Since you only need ½ of the container, you will divide the total cost by 2.

$5.27 / 2 = $2.635

Remember to round up to the nearest penny, making your cost for the yogurt in this recipe $2.64.

You can do this for all the ingredients in all your recipes. This is a fun way to practice some basic math skills for a real life purpose!

GARDEN TO TABLE

Garden Fresh Food

Consider growing some of the veggies that you would use in the recipes included in this book. In many cultures around the world, families rely on the vegetables they grow in their gardens to feed themselves. One of the ways you can differentiate different cultures around the world is by determining the kind of food they grow in their garden.

What people grow determines what they eat. What they grow depends on the soil, the climate, and the geographical area. For example, you are not going to be able to grow the same things in North Dakota that you would be able to grow in Southern Italy. Some plants need hotter weather and longer growing seasons. But no matter where you live or what you want to eat, homegrown vegetables can be far more delicious and much healthier than the ones you buy at the store.

You don't need a lot of space to grow vegetables. Even a five-foot square plot can yield a lot of food!. Check out these great books on gardening to see if this is something you'd like to try:

CHECK OUT THESE GREAT BOOKS ON GARDENING
• The Gardening Book by Jane Bull
• Family Garden by DK Publishing
• Kid's Container Gardening by Cindy Krezel

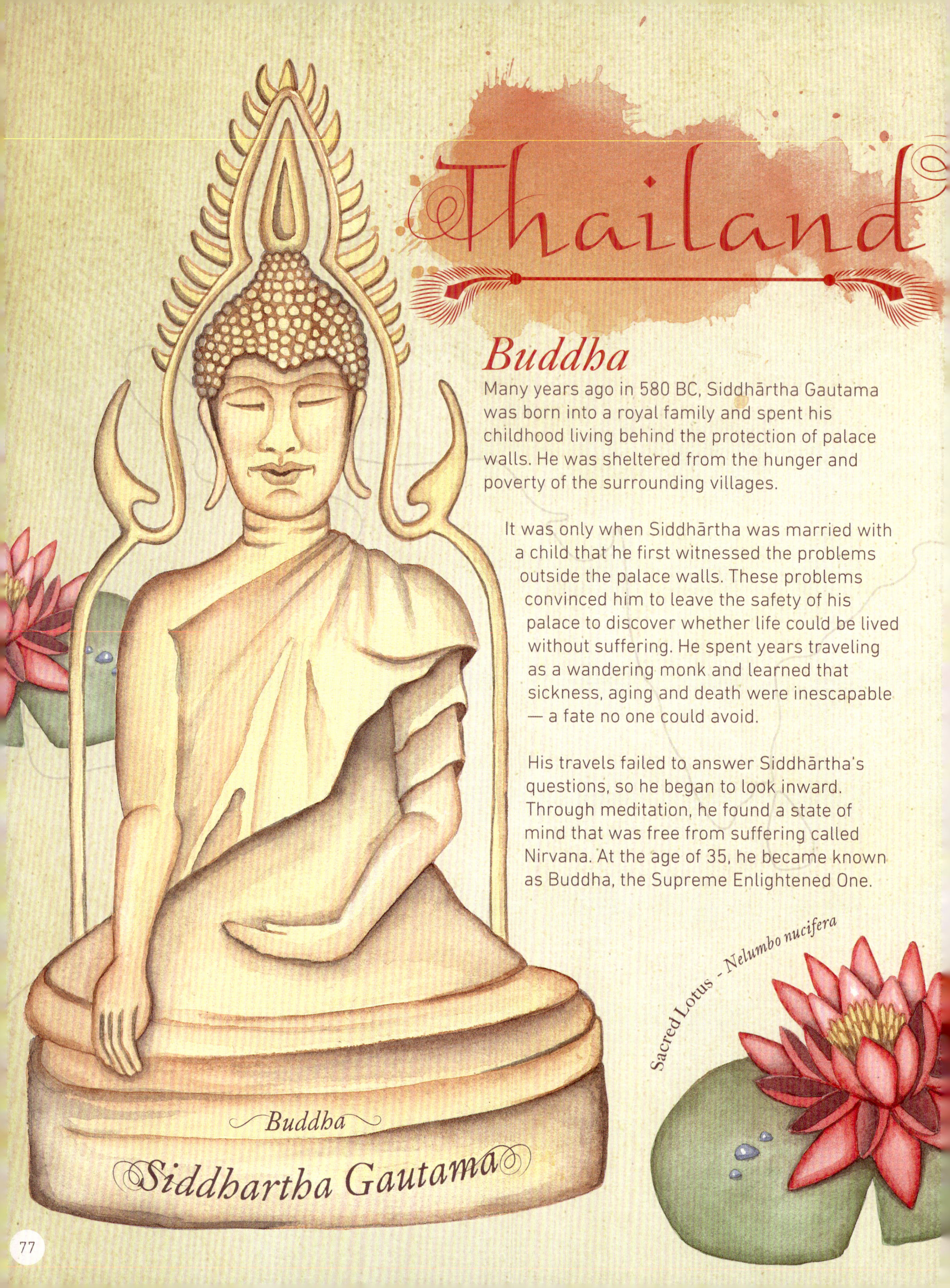

Thailand

Buddha

Many years ago in 580 BC, Siddhārtha Gautama was born into a royal family and spent his childhood living behind the protection of palace walls. He was sheltered from the hunger and poverty of the surrounding villages.

It was only when Siddhārtha was married with a child that he first witnessed the problems outside the palace walls. These problems convinced him to leave the safety of his palace to discover whether life could be lived without suffering. He spent years traveling as a wandering monk and learned that sickness, aging and death were inescapable — a fate no one could avoid.

His travels failed to answer Siddhārtha's questions, so he began to look inward. Through meditation, he found a state of mind that was free from suffering called Nirvana. At the age of 35, he became known as Buddha, the Supreme Enlightened One.

Mango Sticky Rice

(Khao Niaow Ma Muang)

Prepared in kitchens all over Thailand, Mango Sticky Rice is a popular dessert made of rice, sweetened coconut milk and mangoes. Delicious and traditional, this dish is easy to prepare. The most important ingredient is the mangoes, of course. But don't worry if you don't have mangoes in your kitchen. You can prepare this recipe with any other sweet fruit, including peach, papaya, banana, cantaloupe or apricot.

Durian - *Durio kutejensis*

The Spirit House *is a shrine dedicated to the spirits in charge of protecting specific homes or locations in Southeast Asian countries. Spirits can be tricky if they're not happy, so the spirit house provides a place to present offerings.*

Buddhism *is the name of the religion formed by people who choose to live as the Buddha did. These followers try not to do anything bad, to do good deeds and to purify their minds through meditation. Buddhism is practiced all over the world and is the primary religion of Thailand.*

Mango Sticky Rice

STEP BY STEP

1. Prepare rice as directed on packaging.

2. While the rice is cooking, heat the coconut milk until hot; avoid boiling. Stir in sugar and salt until completely dissolved.

3. Place prepared rice in a medium-size mixing bowl and pour half the coconut milk over, saving the rest for later. Evenly distribute the coconut milk through the rice and allow the flavors to blend.

4. Peel the mangoes. (See mango peeling instructions.)

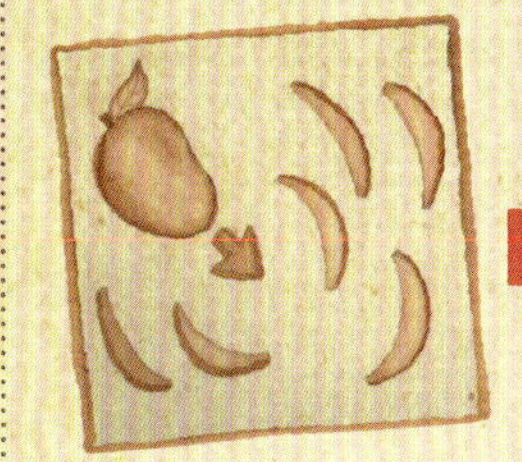

5. Arrange a small mound of sticky rice on individual dessert plates and display the cut mangoes decoratively on top or to the side of the rice. Top with the extra coconut milk mixture.

FROM THE AUTHOR

How to Peel a mango:
With the stem pointing down, cut the mango into three strips from top to bottom. (two outer sides and a smaller mid-section containing the pit) Next, take each of the strips and cut lengthwise and crosswise, forming little cubes. Use a spoon to remove the cubes, and discard the pit.

		% Daily Value
Calories: 730	Calories From Fat 190	
Total Fat: 21g		32%
Saturated Fat: 18g		90%
Trans Fat: 0g		
Cholesterol: 0mg		0%
Sodium: 620mg		26%
Total Carbohydrate: 132g		44%
Dietary Fiber: 9g		36%
Sugars: 73g		
Protein: 10g		

INGREDIENTS

- 3 cups sticky rice (also labeled "glutinous rice" or "sweet rice"), soaked overnight in water or thin coconut milk and drained
- 2 cups canned coconut milk
- 3/4 cup palm sugar, or substitute brown sugar
- 1 teaspoon salt
- 4 ripe mangoes, or substitute sliced ripe peaches or papayas
- Mint or Asian basil sprig

THAILAND

Capital City / Bangkok

Nation Language / Thai

Population / 66,720,153

Currency / Thai baht

Thailand *is called Prathet Thai in the Thai language, which translates to "land of the free." The name makes sense when you consider Thailand is the only region in Southeast Asia that has escaped colonization by European countries.*

The Exotic Fruit of Thailand

Purple Mangosteen: *Garcinia mangostana* - The fruit of the mangosteen is juicy and sweet with a bit of a tangy aftertaste. The outer purple-reddish rind is inedible, leaving only the inner white portion to enjoy. The fruit grows on a tree that is believed to have originated in the Sunda Islands of Indonesia.

Durian: *Durio kutejensis* - This massive fruit (12-15 inches long by 6 inches wide) is known as the "king of the fruits." People are strongly divided as to whether they like the fruit or not because of its pungent aroma. Some say it smells like raw sewage, others say rotting onions. Maybe you should be the judge?

Lychee: *Litchi chinensis* - Lychee is extremely popular in China, Southeast Asia and India where it is grown, as well as countries all over the world where it is exported. The outer portion of the fruit is covered with a bumpy red rind that is not edible. The pulpy flesh inside is fragrant and sweet.

“Cross a river in a crowd and the crocodile won’t eat you.”

Madagascan Proverb, Author Unknown

“Cross a river in a crowd and the crocodile won’t eat you.”

AFRICA
N
E
W
S
EGYPT - MOROCCO - KENYA

The Great City of Alexandria

Alexander the Great founded the ancient city of Alexandria in 331 BC and it grew to become the largest city on the Mediterranean coast. Throughout the city's history, it has been home to many important cultural and historical monuments including the Lighthouse of Alexandria and the Library of Alexandria.

A Library Like None Other

The Library of Alexandria was created to display the wealth of Egypt, showcasing some of the most important historical documents in the world. The ancient library contained rooms designated for the study of fields such as astronomy and medicine. Today it is seen as the inspiration for the modern university campus. At one time, the library even included a zoo set apart for the study of exotic animals. Over the years, several fires and acts of destruction resulted in the loss of many handwritten manuscripts and other irreplaceable treasures. A newly built library exists where the old one once stood.

The Mighty Lighthouse

For centuries the great lighthouse of Alexandria was one of the tallest manmade structures on the planet and is now considered one of the Seven Wonders of the Ancient World. Created in 280 BC to help guide ships from the Mediterranean into the harbor, the lighthouse was eventually destroyed in a series of earthquakes between the years 953 and 1323.

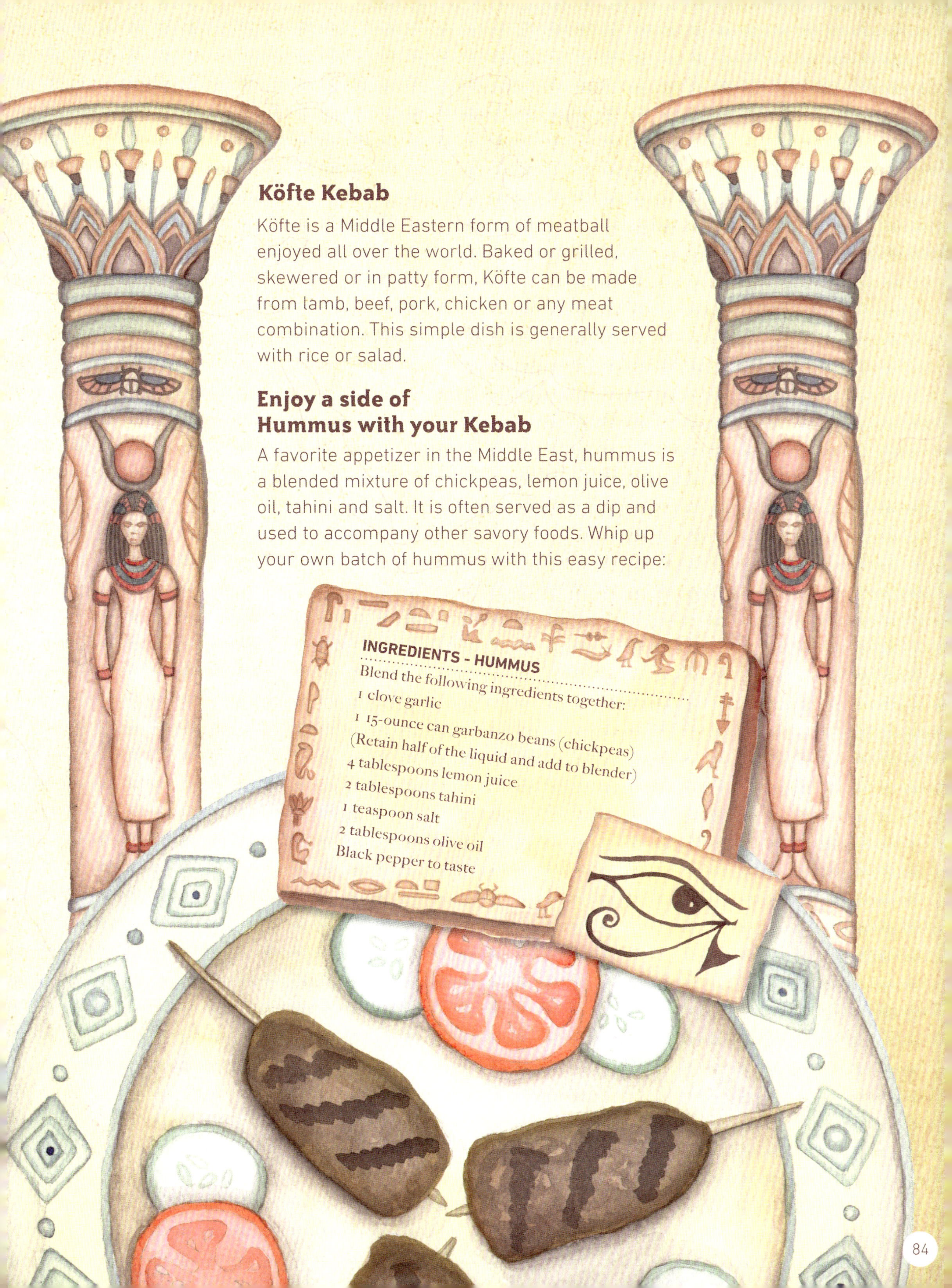

Köfte Kebab

Köfte is a Middle Eastern form of meatball enjoyed all over the world. Baked or grilled, skewered or in patty form, Köfte can be made from lamb, beef, pork, chicken or any meat combination. This simple dish is generally served with rice or salad.

Enjoy a side of Hummus with your Kebab

A favorite appetizer in the Middle East, hummus is a blended mixture of chickpeas, lemon juice, olive oil, tahini and salt. It is often served as a dip and used to accompany other savory foods. Whip up your own batch of hummus with this easy recipe:

INGREDIENTS - HUMMUS

Blend the following ingredients together:

1 clove garlic
1 15-ounce can garbanzo beans (chickpeas)
(Retain half of the liquid and add to blender)
4 tablespoons lemon juice
2 tablespoons tahini
1 teaspoon salt
2 tablespoons olive oil
Black pepper to taste

Köfte Kebab

STEP BY STEP

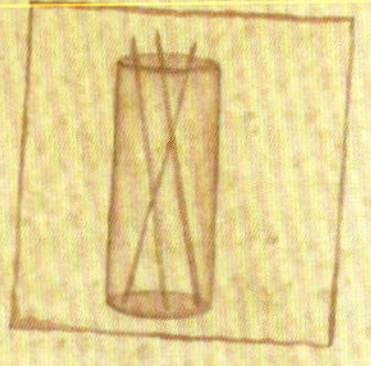

1 Prepare bamboo skewers by soaking them in water for 20 minutes.

2 Mash garlic and salt into a paste using a mortar and pestle. (You can be creative if you don't have a mortar and pestle; try using a rolling pin on a cutting board or the back of a fork.)

3 Mix the garlic and salt paste with ground beef and lamb. Add onion, parsley, black pepper, lemon zest and the rest of the spices. Mix well.

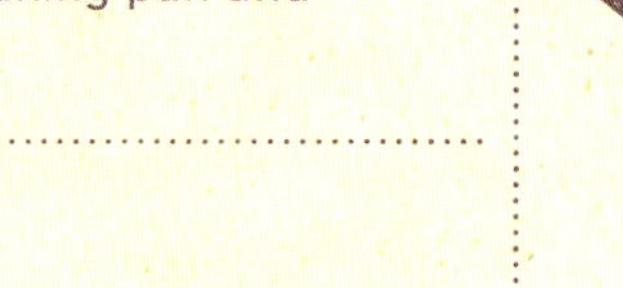

4 Form the mixture into 20 balls. Insert the skewer and flatten the ball into somewhat of an oval shape. The Köfte should be a little off center on the skewer, leaving room to handle later. Place on a foil-lined baking pan and refrigerate at least 30 minutes (up to 12 hours).

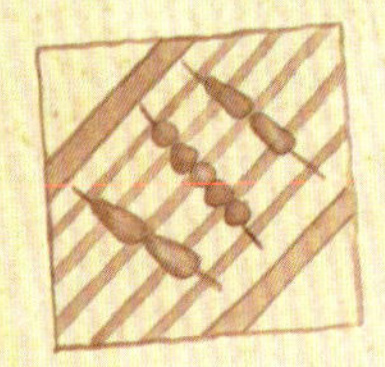

5 Preheat oven to 350 degrees Fahrenheit and bake for 30 minutes. Serve with rice or salad.

SOPHIE'S TIP FOR KIDS

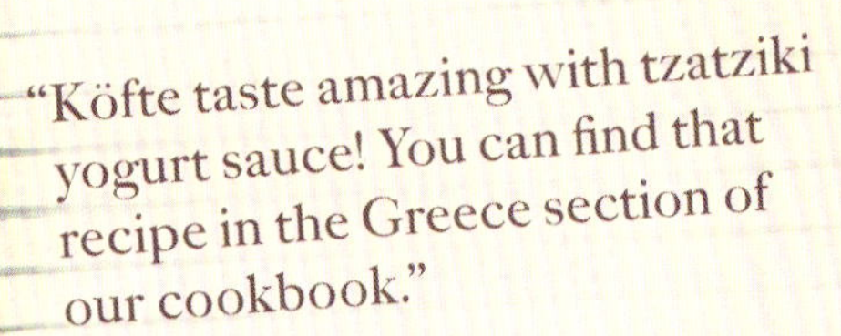

"Köfte taste amazing with tzatziki yogurt sauce! You can find that recipe in the Greece section of our cookbook."

Nutrition Facts : Serving Size: (49g) | Servings: 12

	% Daily Value
Calories: 80 — Calories From Fat 45	
Total Fat: 5g	8%
Saturated Fat: 2g	10%
Trans Fat: 0g	
Cholesterol: 25mg	8%
Sodium: 220mg	9%
Total Carbohydrate: 10g	0%
Dietary Fiber: 0g	0%
Sugars: 0g	
Protein: 7g	

WHAT YOU'LL NEED

INGREDIENTS

- 4 cloves garlic, minced
- 1 teaspoon salt
- 1/2 pound ground lamb
- 1/2 pound ground beef
- 1/2 cup white onion, finely grated
- 1/2 cup chopped fresh parsley
- 1/4 teaspoon ground black pepper
- Zest of 1 lemon
- 20 bamboo skewers

OPTIONAL SPICES

- 1 tablespoon ground coriander
- 1 teaspoon ground cumin
- ½ teaspoon allspice
- ¼ teaspoon cinnamon
- ¼ teaspoon paprika
- ¼ teaspoon ground ginger

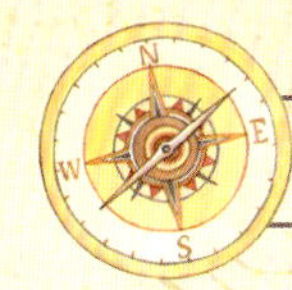

EGYPT

Capital City / Cairo

Nation Language / Arabic

Population / 85,550,000

Currency / Egyptian pound

Egypt *receives irrigation to its farmlands thanks to The Nile River, a very important natural resource. More than 96 percent of Egypt is considered desert because the country receives less than one inch of rain a year.*

Anubis: He Who is Upon His Mountain

Egyptian mythology details the lives of the gods who helped the ancient Egyptians understand their world better. There were more than two thousand gods who held many responsibilities in all planes of existence. Learn more about one of our favorites, Anubis.

Pandalus borealis: *One of the many gifts of the Nile River is a weedy plant called Papyrus. This plant has been used throughout Egyptian history to create everything from baskets and sandals to rope and paper.*

The god of funerals, Anubis was responsible for preparing the soul for the afterlife. He watched over the mummification process to make sure it all went smoothly and assessed those passing through the underworld by placing their hearts on the Scale of Justice.

The Egyptians noticed jackals hanging around the graveyards when their loved ones were recently laid to rest. The people assumed that Anubis favored the pesky creatures, so they began associating the jackal with him. To this day, Anubis is depicted with the head of a jackal and the body of a man.

Morocco
The market of Marrakech is like no other place in the world. Rich with a colorful array of pottery, clothing and spices, the market is a feast for the eyes. It was built in the medina quarter (the central historic part of the city) and has changed little over the thousands of years the market has operated. For this reason, the location has been declared a site of cultural and historical importance.
Souk: An open-air marketplace, or Bazaar filled with market stalls offering many different products.
words you should know
Jamaa el Fna: The large public square in the Medina of Marrakech, around which are situated many souks.
Riad: Historic Moroccan house with many rooms surrounding an internal courtyard. There are many Riad in the Medina of Marrakech.
Indian Cobra - Naja naja

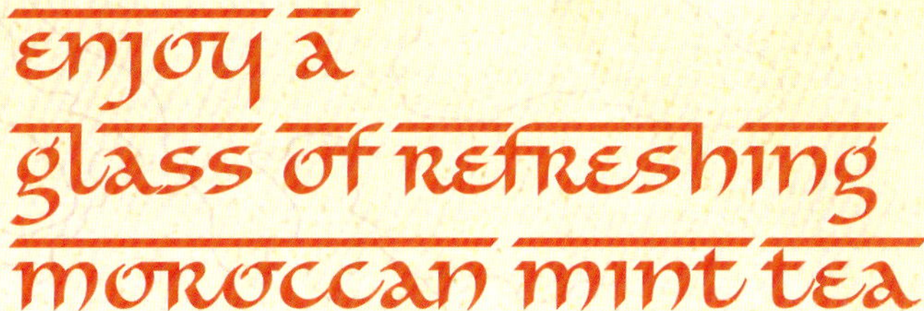

Enjoy a glass of refreshing Moroccan mint tea

- In a medium size kettle, boil at least 4 cups of water (some will evaporate).
- Combine 2 cups hot water, mint, green tea, orange blossom water and sugar in a large teapot and let steep for at least 3 minutes.
- Place a sprig of mint in a medium size drinking glass. Pour tea mixture through a strainer, filling the glass. Enjoy.

INGREDIENTS

1 tablespoon gunpowder green tea leaves
1 large handful fresh spearmint leaves, washed
2 cups boiling water
¼ cup sugar
¼ teaspoon orange blossom water

Mint
Mentha spicata

The Hand of Fatima
This ancient design was originally found in Mesopotamian art and was known as hamsa. It was considered a sign of protection and is found in the paintings, artwork and jewelry of various cultures and religions. Moroccans in Islamic culture called it The Hand of Fatima, a reference to the Prophet Muhammad's daughter Fatima. In Buddhism, the right-hand open palm signifies the Buddha's gesture of teaching and protection.

Stained glass cookies

Even though most Moroccan families serve seasonal fruits after a meal, you know it is time for dessert when the mint tea and cookies arrive at the table. Pastries dripping with honey and smelling of exotic spices like cinnamon, ginger and mint linger heavy in the air.

In every region, patisseries (pastry shops) and market stalls overflow with colorful and aromatic cookies of every shape and size. Moroccans take pride in the food they prepare, both in flavor and presentation, and visitors always find something new to love when dessert is served.

Stained Glass Cookies

STEP BY STEP

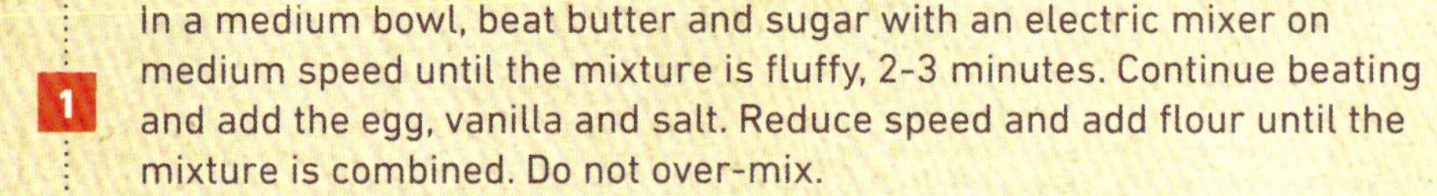

1 In a medium bowl, beat butter and sugar with an electric mixer on medium speed until the mixture is fluffy, 2-3 minutes. Continue beating and add the egg, vanilla and salt. Reduce speed and add flour until the mixture is combined. Do not over-mix.

2 Divide dough in half, shaping into two rounds. Wrap in plastic and refrigerate until firm.

3 Heat oven to 350 degrees Fahrenheit.

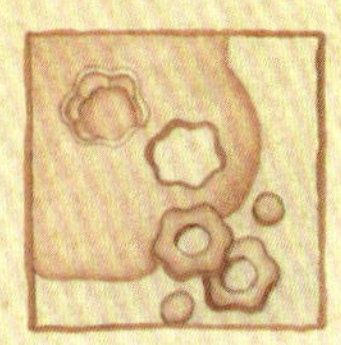

4 Lightly flour your work surface then roll out each piece of dough to 1/8-inch thickness. Cut the dough into interesting shapes using a 2-inch cookie cutter, then place them on a parchment-lined baking sheet. Make sure to space the cookies at least 1-inch apart. Using a second ¾- to 1-inch cookie cutter, cut out the centers from each cookie.

5 Spoon ½ to 1 teaspoon of the crushed candy (depending on the size of the cutout) into the center of each cookie. Bake until the edges are just golden, 7-9 minutes. Cook on the baking sheets for at least 5 minutes, then transfer to wire racks to cool completely.

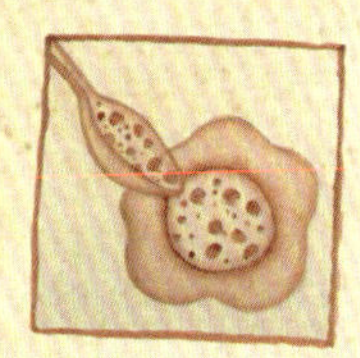

6 Be sure to store the cookies between wax paper sheets in an airtight container.

FROM THE AUTHOR

These cookies also make great Christmas ornaments. Simply poke a small hole all the way through the dough ¼ inch from the edge of the cookie. When the cookie is baked, you can insert a string and tie it off to make a loop suitable for hanging.

Nutrition Facts : Serving Size: (51g) | Servings: 18

	% Daily Value
Calories: 220 — Calories From Fat 70	
Total Fat: 8g	12%
Saturated Fat: 5g	25%
Trans Fat: 0g	
Cholesterol: 30mg	10%
Sodium: 90mg	4%
Total Carbohydrate: 34g	11%
Dietary Fiber: 0g	0%
Sugars: 16g	
Protein: 2g	

WHAT YOU'LL NEED

INGREDIENTS - 3 DOZEN

- 1 1/2 sticks unsalted butter, room temperature
- 3/4 cup sugar
- 1 large egg
- 1 teaspoon vanilla extract
- 3/4 teaspoon kosher salt
- 2 1/2 cups all-purpose flour
- 6-8 ounces colorful hard candies, sorted by color and crushed

MOROCCO

Capital City / Rabat

Nation Language / Arabic

Population / 32,649,130

Currency / Moroccan dirhams

Morocco is situated in the northwest corner of Africa, with the majority of the country's population living in the coastal cities of Fez, Casablanca and Marrakech. The Atlas Mountains and the Sahara Desert dominate the Moroccan landscape.

The Spices of Morocco

Moroccan cooking is known for the many spices that are used to enhance the flavor and fragrance of the food. Spices and herbs are such an important part of Moroccan cuisine, an overwhelming number of market stalls specialize in providing "just right" blends perfect for creating sweet and savory dishes. Below are some of the most common spices used in Morocco.

Cumin: The seeds of the plant *Cuminum cyminum* are used as a spice for their distinctive flavor and aroma. It has been used since ancient times and serves as a staple for many Moroccan homes.

Turmeric: Though it is typically used in a powdered, dry form, fresh turmeric *Curcuma longa* can also be used much like ginger. Turmeric was once known as Indian Saffron because it was cheaper and more widely available than the real saffron.

Paprika: A spice made from ground, dried peppers *Capsicum annuum*, paprika is primarily used to season and color rice, stew and soups.

HERBS AND SPICES OF THE WORLD

For much of recorded history, world civilizations have used herbs and spices for cooking, cleaning and in medicine. Explorers have traveled far and wide to find these prized resources, even going to war over them!

Do you know the difference between herbs and spices? Herbs can be enjoyed fresh or dried and include the leafy parts of a plant, whereas spices are derived from the dried stems, bark, roots, nuts or seeds of a plant. Both herbs and spices give global cuisines their unique and delicious flavors.

Ginseng: *Panax ginseng* (China) Grown only in the cooler climates of the Northern Hemisphere, ginseng is harvested for its thick and fleshy roots, called rhizomes. It is used to make tea, soups and sauces and to flavor vegetables and pork. One variety, Panax quinquefolius, is native to the Appalachian region of the United States.

Star Anise: *Illicium verum* (Vietnam and China) Star anise is the small, woody fruit of a tree in the Magnolia family. Although it smells very much like a spice called anise, the two plants are completely unrelated. Star anise is used to prepare Vietnamese Pho (a noodle and beef broth soup) as well as Chinese Marbled Eggs.

Lavender: *Lavandula angustifolia* (France and England) Lavender is a highly aromatic flower that is used for cooking, potpourri, cosmetics, cleaning products and much more. Originally grown in England and France, lavender is fairly easy to grow and can be cultivated almost everywhere in the world.

Saffron: Crocus sativus (Greece) One of the world's most expensive spices, saffron is used in rice and meat dishes throughout India, Europe, the Middle East, Turkey and elsewhere. Because each crocus blossom only provides a few fragrant strands every season, there is a high demand for the spice, with prices ranging from $500-5,000.00 per pound.
For more info, visit SavorySpiceShop.com
Cinnamon: Cinnamomum verum (India and Sri Lanka) Several tree varieties within the same family produce an aromatic bark that is harvested and sold as cinnamon. Cinnamon is one of the most recognizable spices around the world due to its unique scent. Cooks use the spice primarily in desserts, syrups and curries.
Vanilla: Vanilla planifolia (Mexico) Vanilla comes from the fruit of an exotic orchid vine that originates in parts of Mexico and Guatemala. The fruit pods, commonly called beans, are harvested and cured by hand. Vanilla is used most often in desserts and to enhance the flavor of other ingredients such as chocolate, coffee or caramel.

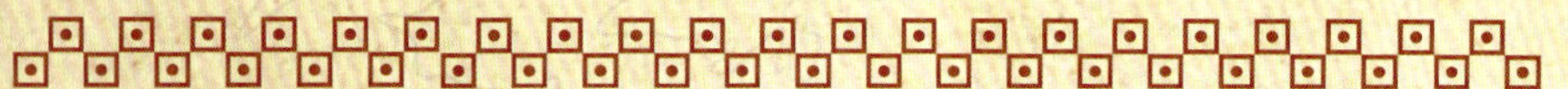

KENYA

African Bush Elephant - *Loxodonta africana*

Acacia Tree

There are few scenes as iconic as the Acacia tree far off in the distance of the Serengeti plains of Kenya and Tanzania, with the sun setting in the background and a tall giraffe feeding on the nutritious leaves of the tree.

Fever Tree - *Acacia xanthophloea*

The Natural Beauty of Kenya

Kenya has a diverse landscape stretching from the Indian Ocean inward toward the endless plains of the Serengeti. The source of the Nile River can be found in Lake Victoria with its world famous Nile crocodiles. The country's namesake, Mount Kenya stretches over 17,000 feet high, making it the second highest peak in Africa.

Kenya is home to some of the most incredible animals in the world, including elephants, lions, giraffes, zebras, antelope, wildebeests and many more. Sadly, hunting and construction in natural habitats once set aside for the animals threatens their very existence. The government and many animal rights organizations are now working to ensure the animals will be around for many years to come.

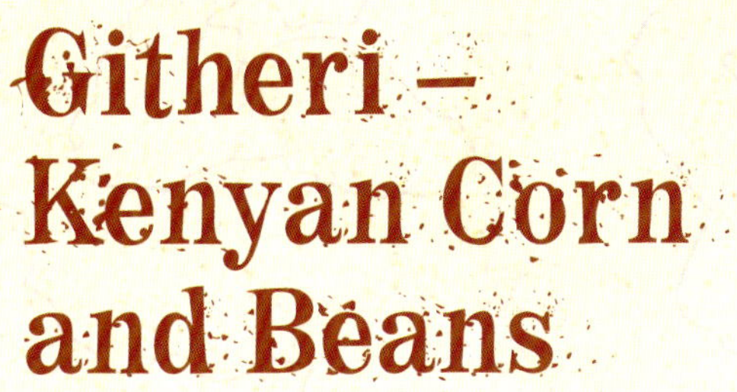

Githeri – Kenyan Corn and Beans

Kenyan cuisine is relatively easy to prepare, both in terms of the number of ingredients and the time it takes to cook. Originating from the Kikuyu tribe in central Kenya, Githeri is one of the most traditional dishes prepared throughout the country.

Traditional Githeri is comprised primarily of corn, beans and tomatoes, making it a very nutritious dish. Historically, Githeri was prepared in clay pots over fire, a process that took many hours. Thanks to modern conveniences the meal can be prepared in no time at all.

Ninapenda twiga, simba, na punda milia

Masai Giraffe - *Giraffa camelopardalis tippelskirchi*

The Maasai Giraffe: *The graceful giraffe is the tallest mammal on the earth and is found in the plains of Kenya. With a neck that stretches almost seven feet tall, the giraffe is able to reach high above other animals to eat the leaves of the Acacia trees.*

Githeri – Kenyan Corn and Beans

STEP BY STEP

1 Heat the vegetable oil in a large pot and sauté the onions and garlic over medium heat until they are lightly cooked, about 3 minutes.

2 Add the curry powder and cook for another minute.

3 Add the kale and reduce the heat to low. Cook, stirring with a wooden spoon until the kale softens, about 10 minutes.

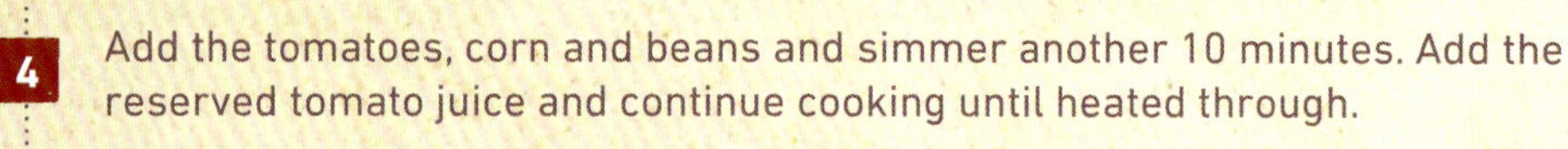

4 Add the tomatoes, corn and beans and simmer another 10 minutes. Add the reserved tomato juice and continue cooking until heated through.

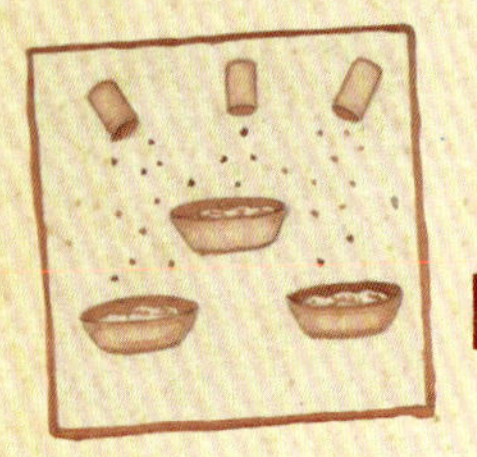

5 Season to your taste with salt and pepper then serve and share! Feel free to personalize your Githeri by adding a few teaspoons of your favorite dried herb such as oregano, thyme or sage.

SOPHIE'S TIP FOR KIDS

"This is a pretty easy recipe to make together as a family. I enjoy helping my little brother prepare Githeri because he can easily measure and pour the ingredients. And he loves stirring the pot while it's cooking!"

Nutrition Facts : Serving Size: (258g) | Servings: 8

	% Daily Value
Calories: 160	Calories From Fat 30
Total Fat: 3.5g	5%
Saturated Fat: 0g	0%
Trans Fat: 0g	
Cholesterol: 0mg	0%
Sodium: 370mg	15%
Total Carbohydrate: 26g	9%
Dietary Fiber: 6g	24%
Sugars: 4g	
Protein: 7g	

INGREDIENTS

- 1 tablespoon vegetable oil
- 1 large onion, chopped
- 3 cloves of garlic, minced
- 1 tablespoon curry powder
- 1 large bunch fresh kale, chopped
- 1 28-ounce can of whole tomatoes, drained, reserve the juice
- 1 15-ounce can whole kernel corn
- 2 cups of cooked beans, any type, drained and rinsed
- Juice of 1 lemon

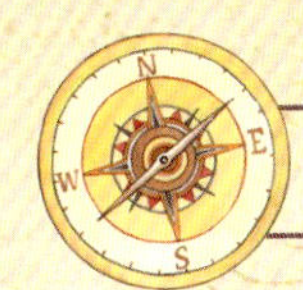

KENYA

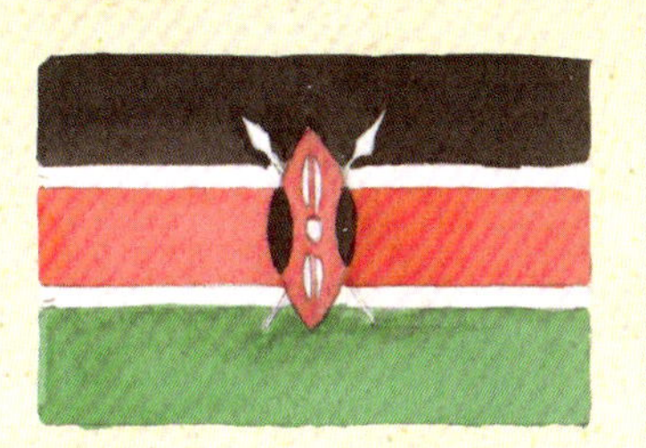

Capital City / Nairobi

Nation Language / Swahili

Population / 44,354,000

Currency / Kenyan Shilling

Kenya is home to more than 450 of some of the earliest fossils belonging to humans, found in the Turkana Basin in Kenya. This evidence leads many scientists to believe the region may have been the birthplace of the original humans.

The Kenyan Maasai

The Maasai are one of the most recognizable and prolific tribes in East Africa. Despite their proximity to modern communities, they still maintain most of their traditional ways and live like their ancestors have for more than 500 years. What started as a small group of warriors with a herd of cattle many years ago has become a large group numbering nearly 900,000 people.

Although the Maasai are known as fierce warriors, the cattle they raise are their most important priority. Raising cattle is an important aspect of the Maasai culture because they believe the rain god Enkai gave all the cattle of the world to them. As you can imagine, this has caused some problems in the past when Maasai found other tribes with cattle. They assumed that the cows must have been stolen from them.

The men of the tribe are responsible for tending the cattle and building thorny fences around the village for protection. Women play an important role in the tribe, having the responsibility of building their homes. Known as Inkajijik, the round huts are built of small tree poles, branches, grass and mud. The entire structure is then covered with cow dung, which when dried, protects and waterproofs the home.

Maasai women are world-famous bead workers, capable of creating vibrantly colored necklaces and clothing. The women of the tribe express their identity and position in society through body painting, piercings, beaded jewelry and brightly colored clothing.

"Aim for the highest cloud so that if you miss it, you will hit a lofty mountain."

Māori Proverb, Author Unknown

OCEANIA
N
E
S
W
NEW ZEALAND

New Zealand

Anna Pavlova was a Russian ballerina with a very successful career in the early 1900s. She was known for her delicate beauty and grace and for being one of the earliest ballerinas to achieve worldwide fame. Can you believe she performed her most famous role in The Dying Swan over 4,000 times during her lifetime? Pavlova was so famous that in 1926 when she toured New Zealand and Australia, everyone wanted a chance to see her perform.

A National Dish

Legend has it that a chef in Wellington, New Zealand was so inspired by her performance, he created a light and airy meringue dessert named in her honor. The dessert has been plagued with controversy ever since. Both Australia and New Zealand claim Pavlova as their "national dish" and have argued about it for decades. While the truth may never be known, some of the earliest references to the dessert suggest the chef in New Zealand was the creator of the delicious treat.

North Island Brown Kiwi: *Apteryx mantelli* - The kiwi is a large, flightless bird about the size of a chicken, with a characteristic long bill. The bird is often seen as a symbol for New Zealand, appearing on military badges, postage stamps and currency. With around 35,000 birds living, the North Island Brown Kiwi is the most common kiwi found in New Zealand. However, because their numbers have decreased greatly in the last 100 years, it is now listed as an endangered species.

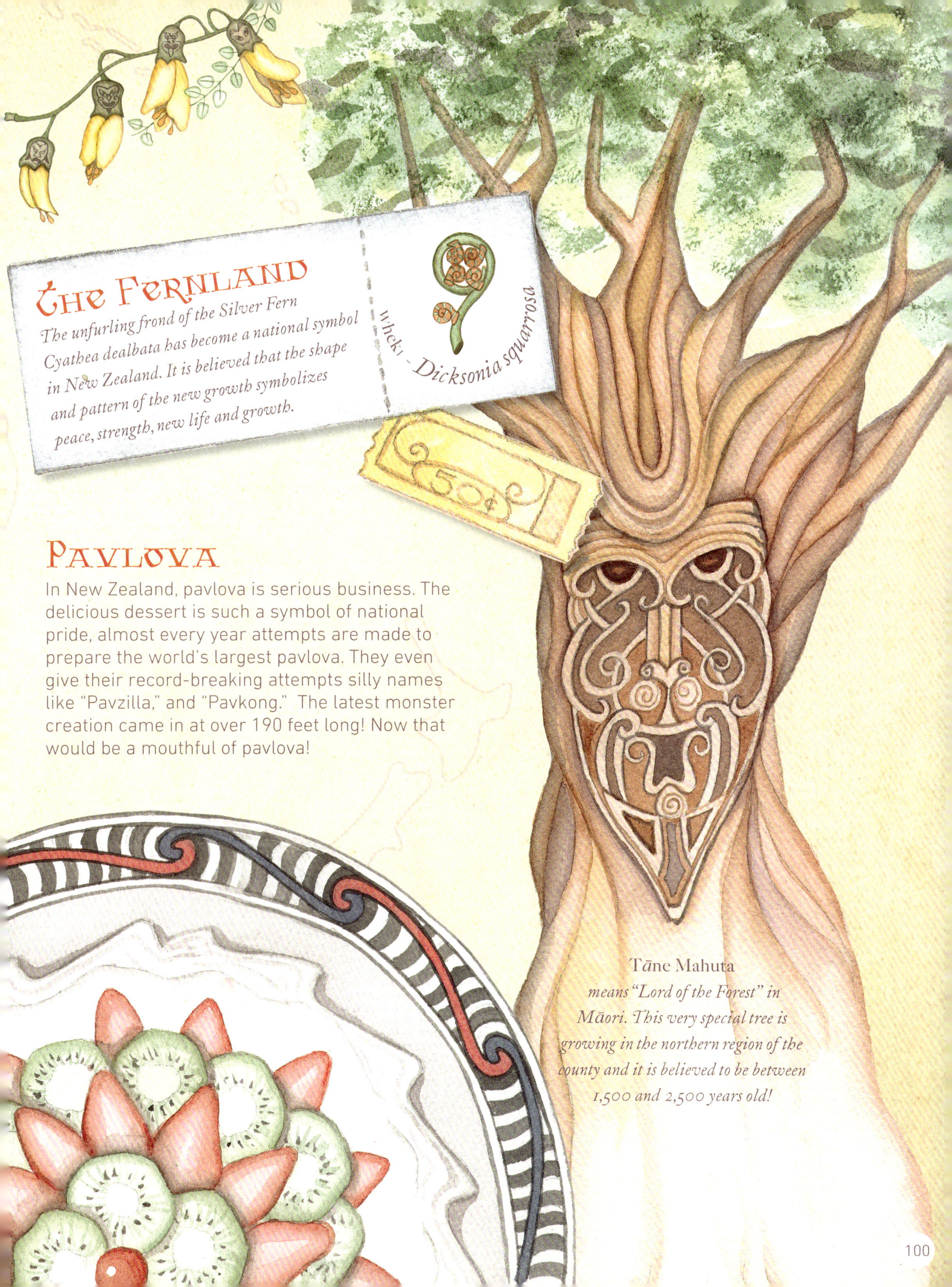

The Fernland

The unfurling frond of the Silver Fern Cyathea dealbata has become a national symbol in New Zealand. It is believed that the shape and pattern of the new growth symbolizes peace, strength, new life and growth.

Pavlova

In New Zealand, pavlova is serious business. The delicious dessert is such a symbol of national pride, almost every year attempts are made to prepare the world's largest pavlova. They even give their record-breaking attempts silly names like "Pavzilla," and "Pavkong." The latest monster creation came in at over 190 feet long! Now that would be a mouthful of pavlova!

Tāne Mahuta
means "Lord of the Forest" in Māori. This very special tree is growing in the northern region of the county and it is believed to be between 1,500 and 2,500 years old!

Pavlova

Step by Step

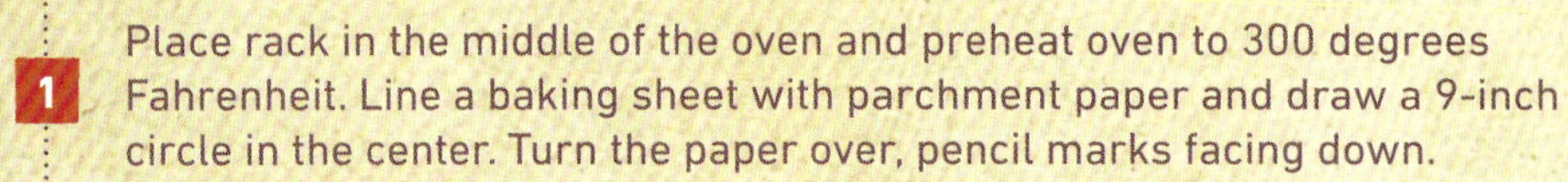

1. Place rack in the middle of the oven and preheat oven to 300 degrees Fahrenheit. Line a baking sheet with parchment paper and draw a 9-inch circle in the center. Turn the paper over, pencil marks facing down.

2. In a large bowl, beat the egg whites until soft peaks form. Continue beating, adding 1 tablespoon of sugar at a time until all of the sugar is incorporated and the mixture becomes thick and glossy. Sprinkle in vanilla extract, lemon juice and cornstarch and fold the ingredients into mixture.

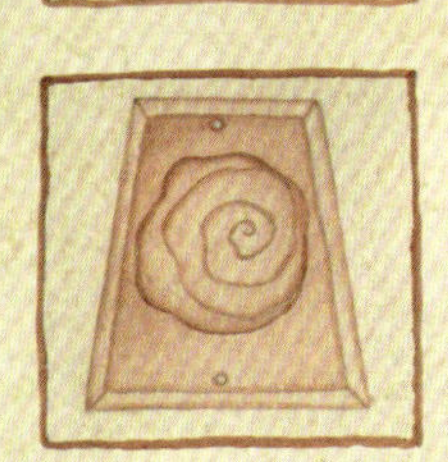

3. With a spatula, transfer mixture into the center of the circle on the parchment paper. From the center, spread the mixture evenly toward the outside edge. Be sure to create a slight depression in the center, building up the edges. This ensures that when it's time to heap on the whipping cream none of it will slide off!

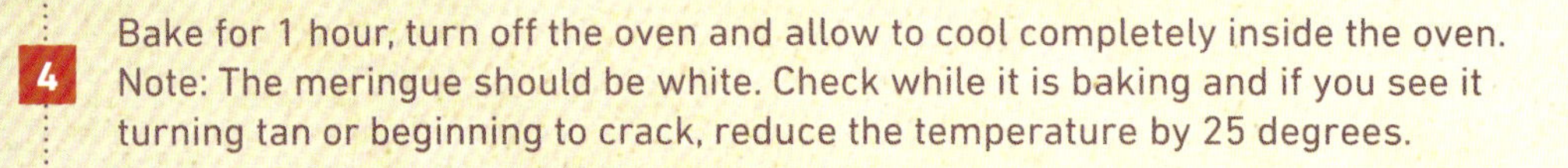

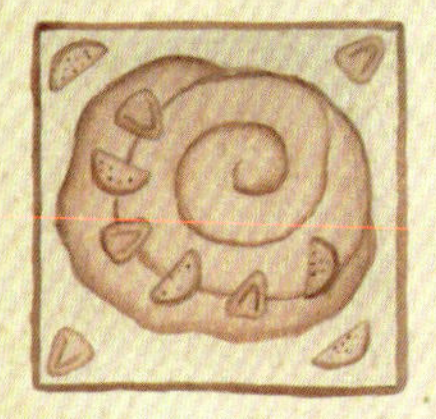

4. Bake for 1 hour, turn off the oven and allow to cool completely inside the oven. Note: The meringue should be white. Check while it is baking and if you see it turning tan or beginning to crack, reduce the temperature by 25 degrees.

5. In a small bowl, beat cream until it begins to form stiff peaks, then set it aside. Prepare the meringue by removing the paper and placing on a dessert plate. Spread whipping cream on top of the dessert in the depression you formed before baking. Top with slices of kiwi and strawberry in any pattern you like.

From the Author

"Pavlova is best served immediately upon placing the fruit and whipped cream. Slice the dessert with a serrated knife. If there are any leftovers, store in an air-tight container."

What You'll Need

Ingredients

- 4 egg whites
- 1 1/4 cups white sugar
- 2 teaspoons cornstarch
- 1 teaspoon vanilla extract
- 1 teaspoon lemon juice
- 1 cup sliced fruit (kiwifruit, strawberries)
- 1 cup lightly sweetened whipped cream

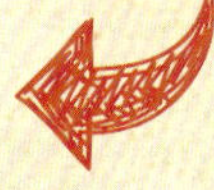

Nutrition Facts : Serving Size: (86g) | Servings: 8

	% Daily Value
Calories: 190	Calories From Fat 45
Total Fat: 4.5g	7%
Saturated Fat: 3g	15%
Trans Fat: 0g	
Cholesterol: 15mg	5%
Sodium: 35mg	1%
Total Carbohydrate: 34g	11%
Dietary Fiber: 0g	0%
Sugars: 33g	
Protein: 2g	

NEW ZEALAND

Capital City / Wellington

Nation Language / English

Population / 4,365,113

Currency / New Zealand Dollar

New Zealand is the product of volcanic activity as massive undersea eruptions created both the North and South Islands over many years. The island nation has more than 50 volcanoes, some of which are still active.

The Golden Kawhai – A Folk Tale of the Māori People

Sophora microphylla, known as Kōwhai (meaning "yellow" in Māori) is a small tree with bright yellow flowers that is commonly found in most parts of New Zealand. This story explains how the tree came to be.

Many years ago, before the Europeans came to New Zealand, a young couple sat beneath a tree bare of leaves or flowers. It was clear the two were in love – they had spent every moment together for weeks. And, now it was time for the young man to ask the young lady for her hand in marriage. But, her answer surprised him.

"I can only marry a man who can perform great and unexplained miracles," she said. The young man was stunned for a moment. "You shall see what I can do," he said simply. With no motion at all, he spoke ancient and mysterious words aloud. For a second the two starred at one another, saying nothing. Then with a wink of his eye, he stood to his feet and commanded, "Great dormant tree, I command you to flower before our eyes!" With that, the tree erupted into a great, wild mass of golden flowers. The young girl had no choice but to say yes.

The Māori People

The Māori are the indigenous, or native, people of New Zealand. Over 1,250 years ago, Polynesian explorers travelled the South Pacific in giant canoes and when they happened across the shores of New Zealand decided to stay. In 1769, when the British explorer Captain James Cook first visited New Zealand, he estimated there were over 150,000 Māori people living in the region.

The Māori people have strong cultural and religious beliefs involving nature. They believe there are many different gods who are represented by the sky, the earth, flowers, forests and even the forces of nature. They celebrate and give thanks to their gods through song and dance, and special masks and carvings.

ANIMALS OF THE WORLD

Scientists who study animals are called zoologists. Throughout history, they have recorded more than 20,000 species of fish, 6,000 species of reptiles, 9,000 birds, 1,000 amphibians, and over 15,000 species of mammals! The list of animals that share our planet with us is incredible! How many different species of animals can you think of?

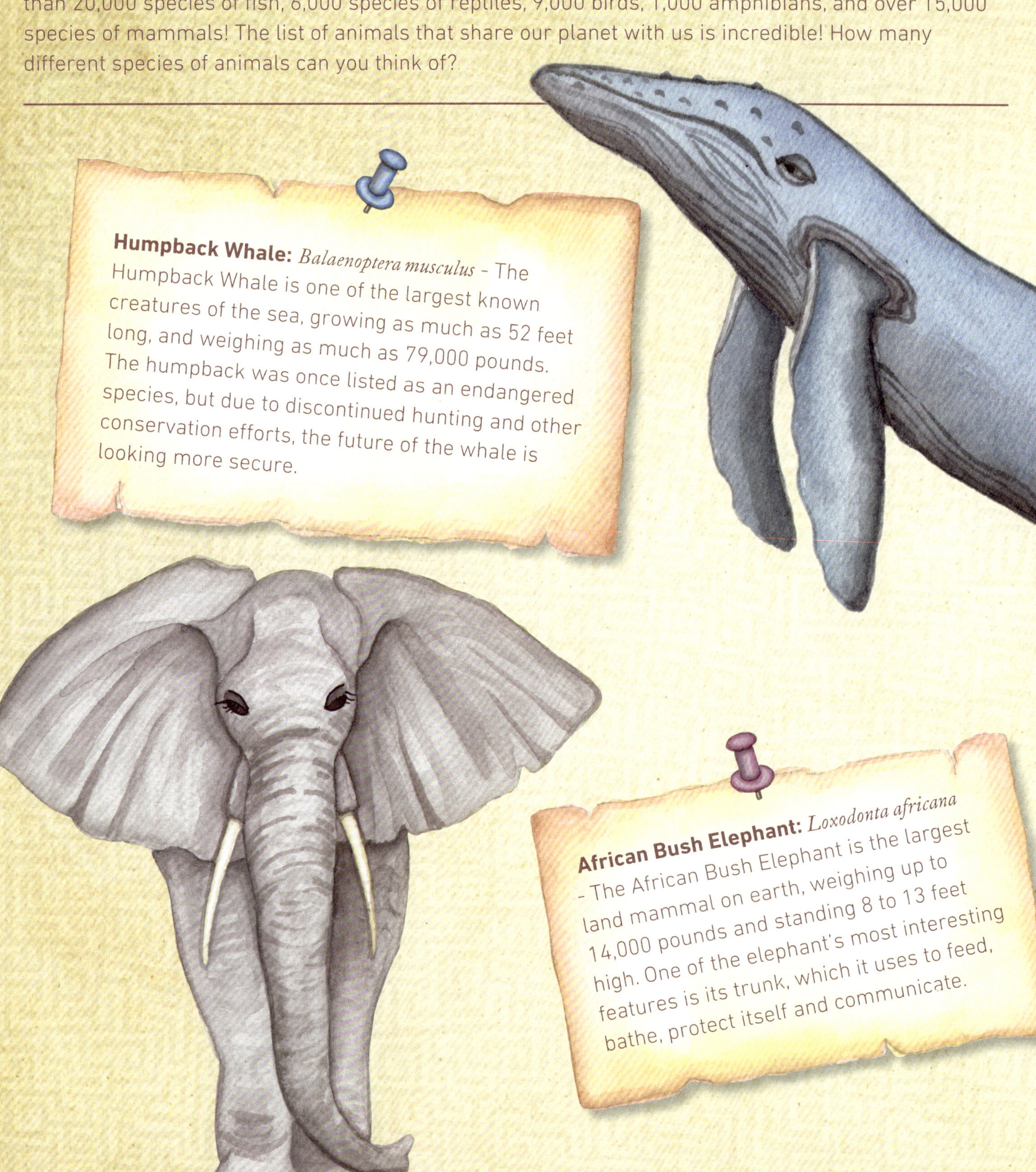

Humpback Whale: *Balaenoptera musculus* - The Humpback Whale is one of the largest known creatures of the sea, growing as much as 52 feet long, and weighing as much as 79,000 pounds. The humpback was once listed as an endangered species, but due to discontinued hunting and other conservation efforts, the future of the whale is looking more secure.

African Bush Elephant: *Loxodonta africana* - The African Bush Elephant is the largest land mammal on earth, weighing up to 14,000 pounds and standing 8 to 13 feet high. One of the elephant's most interesting features is its trunk, which it uses to feed, bathe, protect itself and communicate.

Red Kangaroo : *Macropus rufus* - The Red Kangaroo is the largest of the marsupial animals, known to carry their young in an external pouch. When the female kangaroo gives birth to a single baby the size of a cherry, it crawls into her pouch where it stays for two months. During this time, the baby kangaroo (known as a joey) continues to mature. At eight months of age, the joey leaves the pouch for good.

Indian Cobra: *Naja naja* - The Indian Cobra is a highly venomous snake known for its use by snake charmers. One of the most impressive characteristics of the snake is its hood, which is created as the animal's ribs separate in its neck when it feels threatened.

African Lion : *Panthera leo* - Considered one of the strongest and most courageous mammals of the animal kingdom, the African Lion is found in regions south of the Sahara Desert in Africa. These big cats of the African grasslands feed on antelopes, zebras, wildebeest and other large animals that cross its path.

HOW TO INCORPORATE THIS BOOK INTO THE CLASSROOM

This is more than a list of lesson plans; it is a springboard for your own unique style of teaching based on the students you have in your classroom this year. All the activities and ideas are aligned with the Common Core State Standards for English Language Arts using both literary and informational text.

The National Council of Teachers of English believes that literacy growth begins before children enter school as they experience and experiment with literacy activities: reading and writing and associating spoken words with their graphic representations.

This book also supports the NCTE Standards for English Language Arts:

- Read texts to acquire new information.
- Apply a wide range of strategies to comprehend, interpret and appreciate texts.
- Conduct research on interests by generating ideas and questions, and gather, evaluate, and synthesize data from a variety of sources.
- Read texts to build an understanding of oneself and the world's cultures.
- Develop an understanding of and respect for diversity in language use, patterns and dialects across cultures, ethnic groups, geographic regions and social roles.

Use your imagination and resources to come
up with other great ideas of your own!

Grades K-2

Focus Activity:
Have students create a "T Chart" listing their favorite foods on one side and foods they might not like as well on the other. Help them locate some of their favorites in the ingredients lists from the recipes. This could be the basis for many different types of activities or lessons across the curriculum. For social studies, you could show familiar cross-cultural characteristics. In reading, you could create a comprehension lesson using compare/contrast skills. For math, a graphing activity could focus on "which cultures use how many of your favorite ingredients?"

Other Ideas:
— Use this resource as a picture book. Read aloud the vignettes from each country to encourage curiosity about different cultures around the world.

— Use the rich visual format of this book to engage children in recognizing colors, shapes, numbers, amounts, letters, letter sounds and words.

Grade 3

Focus Activity:
To help students rethink text in a different genre, create or locate a Found Poetry activity where they can spend some time locating words or phrases from a section of The Cultured Chef. Perhaps they will create a poem around gardening, art or music. Or they might choose any of the represented cultures. After students choose words and phrases that appeal to them, they can create a line for a class poem to which everyone contributes.

Other Ideas:
— After students choose one of the cultures represented in the book, have them create a KWL chart to guide their thinking and learning. Students can research the country they chose and fill out the chart as they go. If you want to encourage students to continue their learning and becoming experts, they could write reports, create presentations, etc.

— In some school districts across the nation, third graders participate in a "Culture Fair." For this project, they begin researching the culture of their heritage at the beginning of the year, adding to their knowledge as time goes on. In the spring, the students convene in an agreed upon area to display their presentations of learning.

HOW TO INCORPORATE THIS BOOK INTO THE CLASSROOM

Grade 4

Focus Activity:

Incorporate the gardening pages by having students learn about helpful and harmful insects. In groups, students could brainstorm short lists of bugs they've seen in vegetable or flower beds. Then they could each choose an insect for research to determine what the different functions of these bugs are in gardens and how they affect plants and other aspects of a "growing habitat." Expert group share-out presentations could include posters, PowerPoint presentations or other creative visuals.

Other Ideas:

— The above activity could be a springboard to other science topics such as heredity, adaptation, behaviors and structure; it integrates more than one discipline (reading, writing, science, technology and/or art) into the activity.

— A focus on science could include many geography and ecosystems activities with emphasis on climates, terrains and growing seasons. A focus question for many of these activities could be, "How does the geography of a place affect the culture of that region?"

Grade 5

Focus Activity:

Use this book to help students understand units of measure. Have students choose recipes in the book that sound interesting and delicious to them. Ask them to write down how many cups, for example, of an ingredient is needed. Then ask them to convert that measurement to pints or fluid ounces. You can extend this activity by asking students to find equivalencies in many different units of measure. Bonus: Because most countries use a different system of measurement, have students convert their standard measurements to metric.

Other Ideas:

— Use the "How Much Will It Cost?" activity on page 75 as a classroom math project. Have students create the recipe and enjoy it in class afterward.

— Recipes are a natural for teaching and understanding fractions. Use those found in this book to connect your math lessons to social studies or science content you may also be teaching.

— Write word problems based on the recipes and/or vignettes in the book.

MULTICULTURAL READING LIST

PreK

- Grandmother's Nursery Rhymes by Nelly Palacio Jaramilo
- Margaret and Margarita by Lynn Reiser
- I Love My Hair by Natasha Tarpley
- Baby Rattlesnake by Te Ata
- We're Roaming in the Rainforest by Laurie Krebs
- How Many Seeds in a Pumpkin? By Margaret McNamara

Primary

- Drumbeat... Heartbeat: A Celebration of the Powwow by Susan Braine
- Halmoni and the Picnic by Sook Nyul Choi
- From the Bellybutton of the Moon: and Other Summer Poems by Francisco X. Alarcon
- The People Could Fly: American Black Folktales by Virginia Hamilton
- Senorita Gordita by Helen Ketteman
- The Eclipse by Nicholas Beatty
- Horse Songs: The Naadam of Mongolia by Ted and Betsy Lewin
- Martina the Beautiful Cockroach: A Cuban Folktale by Carmen Agra Deedy
- When Turtle Grew Feathers: A Tale from the Choctaw Nation by Tim Tingle

Intermediate

- Baseball Saved Us by Ken Mochizuki
- John Henry by Julius Lester
- Tar Beach by Faith Ringgold
- Bud, Not Buddy by Christopher Paul Curtis
- The Birchbark House by Louise Erdrich
- Esperanza Rising by Pam Munoz Ryan
- The Rainbow People by Laurence Yep
- The Night the Animals Danced by Nicholas Beatty
- Quilted Landscape: Conversations with Young Immigrants by Yale Strom
- I Lay My Stitches Down: Poems of American Slavery by Cynthia Grady
- Same Sun Here by Silas House and Neela Vaswani
- The Boy Who Harnessed the Wind by William Kawamba and Bryan Mealer

Middle School

- Roll of Thunder, Hear My Cry by Mildred D. Taylor
- The Friends by Kazumi Yumoto
- Bless Me, Ultima by Rudolfo A. Anaya
- Copper Sun by Sharon Draper
- All the Broken Pieces by Ann E. Burg
- Mare's War by Tanita S. Davis
- Alligator Bayou by Donna Jo Napoli
- Dragonwings by Laurence Yep

High School

- Bitter Melon by Cara Chow
- The House on Mango Street by Sandra Cisneros
- Code Talker by Joseph Bruchac
- Does My Head Look Big In This? by Randa Abdel-Fattah
- The Orange Houses by Paul Griffin
- The Absolutely True Diary of a Part-time Indian by Sherman Alexie
- Black, White, Other by Joan Steinau Lester
- Color of the Sea by John Hamamura

SKILL LEVELS

In other countries, children do a lot of food preparation and cooking. Generally, this is because families have to share a tremendous workload. Often domestic chores will be left to kids while parents work in the fields, herd animals or even leave the home to work in another location. All children are capable and can be taught many skills at an early age. Here are some skills and tasks that young cooks and growing cooks can master:

2 Year Olds

Children want to help at a very early age. When you work with your child in the kitchen, safety is key. Very small children can stay close to you, watch you cook and help in the following ways:

- Wash their hands
- Wipe off counter tops
- Wash fruits and veggies (you can teach them the names of the foods while they wash.)
- Stir batter or other ingredients in bowls
- Mash ingredients with forks or mashers

3-5 Year Olds

Children have widely varied ability levels at these ages. You will be the best judge of which skills your child should try to master first.

- Knead and shape dough
- Grease pans
- Using cookie cutters
- Open packages
- Peel oranges or hard-cooked eggs
- Tear herbs, lettuces, and other leafy veggies
- Spreading peanut butter, butter, and other spreads on bread or dough

5-7 Year Olds

As children get a little older, the skills they are able to master become a little more complex. Always remember to keep an eye on your kiddos in the kitchen, especially when they begin using cutting utensils.

- Measure ingredients
- Cut soft foods with a blunt or plastic knife
- Set the table
- Snip herbs with "school" scissors
- Garnish food
- Making pie crusts and scones by rubbing in flour and butter using fingertips
- Beat eggs or batters with a whisk

8-10 Year Olds

These are the ages where you will begin to let children work with a little more independence. Continue to monitor their safety, giving pointers and tips where needed. Let them problem-solve and plan more at this age to encourage engagement.

- Help plan the meal
- Find ingredients in cupboards, fridge, or spice rack
- Open cans
- Use a peeler, garlic press, and hand grater
- Boil eggs
- Use the microwave, with supervision
- Begin using knives, with supervision
- Make a salad

11-12 Year Olds

At this age, children tend to rush through activities they have done before. Your child may feel s/he is completely capable of all kitchen work at this stage, but when introducing new skills and equipment, continue to provide careful supervision.

- Use a microwave oven
- Prepare simple recipes with few ingredients
- Roast vegetables
- Melt chocolate in the microwave
- Use a hand mixer
- Steam rice
- Begin using the stove and oven, with supervision
- Fry eggs
- Grill sandwiches
- Cook pancakes
- Make soup

13-16 Year Olds

Older cooks like to experiment with recipes and presentation. Allow lots of creativity — while reminding them not to vary the recipes too much — and continue to use safe habits.

- Prepare recipes with multiple ingredients
- Prepare recipes independently
- Safely use kitchen appliances
- Marinate foods
- Bake yeast doughs and pastries

MEASUREMENT & SUBSTITUTION GUIDE

MEASURING CONVERSIONS

Pinch = 1/16
Dash = 1/8 teaspoon or less
3 teaspoons = 1 tablespoon
2 tablespoons = 1/8 cup or 1 ounce
4 tablespoons = 1/4 cup
5 1/3 tablespoons = 1/3 cup
8 tablespoons = 1/2 cup
16 tablespoons = 1 cup
1 cup = 8 fluid ounces
2 cups = 1 pint = 16 fluid ounces
4 cups = 2 pints = 1 quart = 32 fluid ounces
2 quarts = 1/2 gallon = 1.89 liters
4 quarts = 1 gallon
1 oz. = 28.35 grams
1 liter = 1.06 quarts

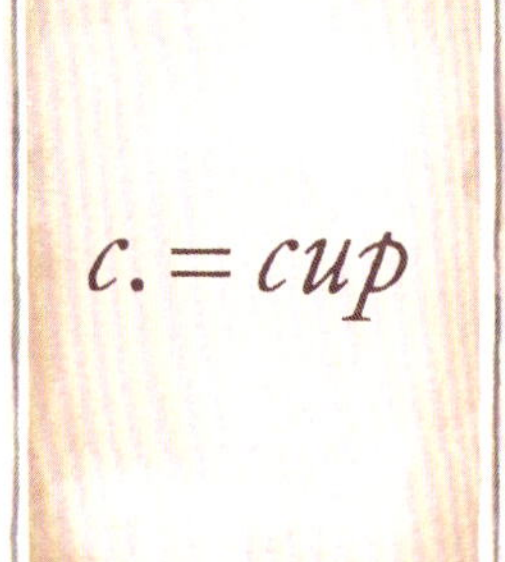

T. = tablespoon

t. = teaspoon

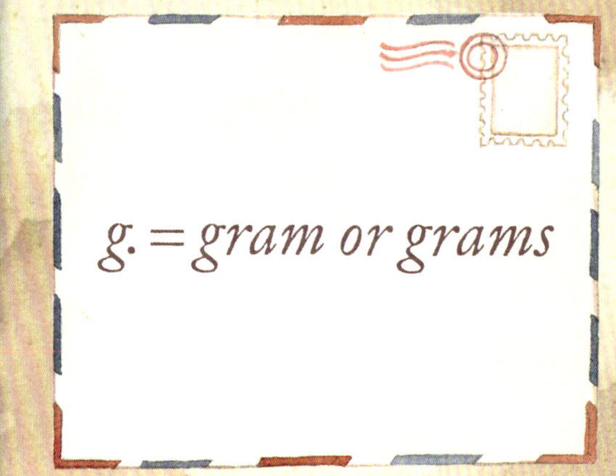

lb. = pound

pt. = pint

oz = ounce

qt. = quart

INGREDIENT SUBSTITUTIONS

1 cup all-purpose flour - 1/2 cup all-purpose flour + 1/2 cup whole wheat flour
1 cup all-purpose flour - 1 cup + 2 Tbsp. cake flour
1 cup cake flour - 7/8 cup (1 cup minus 2 Tbsp.) all-purpose flour + 2 Tbsp. corn starch
1 cup self-rising flour - 1 cup cake or all-purpose flour + 1 1/2 tsp. baking powder + 1/2 tsp. salt
1 cup self-rising cornmeal - 3/4 cup + 3 Tbsp. white or yellow cornmeal+ 1 Tbsp. baking powder + 1/2 tsp. salt
1 pkg. (1/4 oz.) active dry yeast - 2 1/4 tsp. (1/4 oz.) fast-rising yeast or 1 (1/2 oz.) cake compressed yeast
1 tsp. baking powder - 1 tsp. baking soda + 1/2 tsp. cream of tartar
1 cup honey - 1 1/4 cups sugar or 2 cups powdered sugar + 1/4 cup liquid
1 cup whole milk - 1 cup skim milk + 2 Tbsp. melted butter or margarine
1 cup sour cream or crème fraiche - 1 cup 2% or 10% plain Greek-style yogurt
1 Tbsp. cornstarch - 2 Tbsp. all-purpose flour or 4 tsp. quick-cooking tapioca
1 cup packed brown sugar - 1 cup white granulated sugar creamed with 2 Tbsp. molasses
1 ounce unsweetened chocolate - 3 Tbsp. unsweetened cocoa plus 1 Tbsp. shortening
1 large egg - 1 Tbsp. milled flax + 3 Tbsp. water or 1/4 cup soft tofu

This information has been provided by the Home Baking Association, HomeBaking.org

SPECIAL THANKS

Special thanks to our friends, family and financial backers who championed our cause. We are grateful you recognized the need for learning about other cultures and helped make The Cultured Chef become reality.

Our Supporters Who Went Out Of Their Way To Make This Book Possible:

Jeannie and Dave McIntyre
Richard and Darlene Beatty
Mark Middleton
Lois Middleton
Jonathan Swanson
Russell J. Young
Matt Watson
Brian D'Angelo
Cindy Okumoto
Pamela Ellgen
Rachelle Matheson
Kimberly Field
Nancy DeLong
Pam Atherton
Erika Albright
Bruin Albright
Sophie Albright
Todd Werkhoven
Donna Stevens
Cole Stoddard
Jim Lattazanio
Precision Images
Jackie Welch
Kurt and Audrey Saberi
Counterform Graphic Design
Charlene Patton
Jana Patton
Sharon Davis
Paula Marra
Barbara Ross
Carrie Habrich
Sarah Dooley
Steven Rentz
Derek Ladd
Marc A. Beemer
Frank and Pat Carroll
Richard J. Lord
Arthur Wegg
George Green
Erica Toelle
Jill Marie Ramos
Amanda Furbee
Mark J. Barrett
Kohel Haver
Jessica Harkin
Candace Montgomery
Rob McCaig

Photo By: Juli Buck

Contributing Editor, Rachelle Matheson

Rachelle Matheson is an educator living in Washington State with her husband, four children and two cats. The Cultured Chef marks her first contribution to children's literature.

Contributing Editor, Sophie Albright

Sophie Albright is a 10-year-old student living with her family in Washington State. She first developed an interest in cooking when she tested recipes for Nicholas and Coleen's first book, Baking with Friends.

Editor, Pamela Ellgen

Pamela Ellgen is a food writer and editor based in Los Angeles, where she lives with her husband and two sons. She loves surfing, shopping the farmer's markets and soaking up the California sunshine.

Dietitian, Jana Patton

Jana Patton is a Registered Dietitian with the Riley County Health Department in Manhattan, Kansas. She is a graduate of Kansas State University with two degrees in Nutritional Sciences and Dietetics.

ABOUT US

Author - Nicholas Beatty has remained consistent throughout his career in his dedication to exploring the importance of family. As a children's author, documentary photographer and youth mentor, his footprint has been one of proclaiming the importance of a happy childhood. A native of the Northwest, Nicholas spends his time traveling the world in search of great stories.

Nicholas Beatty

Photo By: Russell J. Young

Illustrator - Coleen McIntyre graduated from the University of the Arts in Philadelphia with a BFA in Illustration. Proclaiming a love for watercolor, Coleen also incorporates gouache, ink and other mediums if the illustration calls for it. A native of New Jersey, she found the inspiration she needed in the beauty of the Pacific Northwest where she now calls home.

Coleen McIntyre

Photo By: Russell J. Young

ADVANCE PRAISE FOR THE CULTURED CHEF

Dr. Susan Bartell, Nationally Recognized Psychologist and Author of ***Dr. Susan's Fit And Fun Family***

"At its core, ***The Cultured Chef*** supports one of the most important bonds — a healthy and nurturing relationship between parent and child."

Nancy Baggett, Award-Winning Author of ***Simply Sensational Cookies***

"Visually stunning, and carefully and thoughtfully produced, this charming, unusual book opens up children's eyes to an array of the world's cultures and cuisines."

Father Dominic, Television Host of ***Breaking Bread***, and Author of ***The Breadhead Bible***

"Exposure to world cultures, diversity education, kitchen techniques, folklore, history, the arts — ***The Cultured Chef*** is an educator's dream come true!"

Jennie Schacht, IACP Award-Nominated Author of ***Southern Italian Desserts***

"Beatty and McIntyre's comprehensive exploration of world culture through the universal lens of food is vibrant and inviting."

Pam Atherton, Host of ***A Closer Look*** Radio

"***The Cultured Chef*** takes children around the world through recipes and stories, fostering cultural development and diversity using the global language of food."

Sharon Davis, Author of ***Baking With Friends***

"***The Cultured Chef*** is just the kind of "compass" I love to use while teaching family and food education programs, workshops and community activities."

Charlene Patton
Executive Director, Home Baking Association

"Without leaving home, readers can travel and explore the cuisine of other countries right in their own kitchen with this delightful book!"